Foundations for Violence-Free Living
A Step-by-Step Guide to Facilitating Men's Domestic Abuse Groups

created by the Wilder Men's Domestic Abuse Program

written by David J. Mathews, MA, LICSW

Amherst H. Wilder Foundation
Saint Paul, Minnesota

We thank the Bigelow Foundation of St. Paul, Minnesota,
for their contribution toward the development of this curriculum.

This guidebook and accompanying participant's workbook were developed by the Community Assistance Program (CAP), a program of the Amherst H. Wilder Foundation in St. Paul, Minnesota. CAP is one of the largest and most comprehensive domestic abuse programs in the country. Staff provide crisis intervention counseling, information and referral, advocacy and assessments for women, men, teens, and children who call for assistance in dealing with family violence. The Bigelow Foundation of St. Paul, Minnesota, helped underwrite the development of this curriculum.

The Amherst H. Wilder Foundation is one of the largest and oldest endowed human service agencies in America. For more than eighty years, the Wilder Foundation has provided human services responsive to the welfare needs of the community, all without regard to or discrimination on account of nationality, sex, color, or religious practice.

If you would like to know more about the Wilder Community Assistance Program and its services for survivors and perpetrators of violence, contact:

Community Assistance Program
650 Marshall Avenue
St. Paul, Minnesota 55104
Phone (612) 221-0048

We hope you find this curriculum helpful! To purchase additional copies or get information on other Foundation publications, please see the order form in the back of this book or contact:

Amherst H. Wilder Foundation
Publishing Center
919 Lafond Avenue
St. Paul, Minnesota 55104
Phone toll free 1 (800) 274-6024

Curriculum developed by the staff of Wilder Community Assistance Program
Written by David J. Mathews
Edited by Vincent Hyman
Designed by Rebecca Andrews
Cover illustration by Greg Preslicka

Manufactured in the United States of America

Library of Congress Cataloging-in-Publication Data

Mathews, David J.
    Foundations for violence-free living : a step-by-step guide to facilitating men's domestic abuse groups / created by the Wilder Men's Domestic Abuse Program ; written by David J. Mathews.
        p.   cm.
    ISBN 0-940069-05-9
    1. Abusive men--Counseling of.   2. Social work with men--Problems, exercises, etc.   3. Social group work--Problems, exercises, etc.   4. Abusive men--Psychology.   5. Wife abuse--Prevention.   I. Men's Domestic Abuse Program (Saint Paul, Minn.)   II. Title.
HV6626.M4   1995   95-36815
362.82'928--dc20

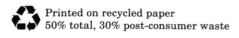
Printed on recycled paper
50% total, 30% post-consumer waste

About the Author

David J. Mathews, MA, LICSW, is a counselor with the Amherst H. Wilder Foundation Community Assistance Program in St. Paul, Minnesota, and a therapist with the Judson Family Center in Minneapolis. He is very active in violence intervention and prevention in communities and schools in the St. Paul metropolitan area, and has consulted with and trained local, state, and national organizations. He is the author of numerous presentations, a chapter on parenting groups for men who batter, and a collection of parenting activities, *Parenting Under Stress*. Mr. Mathews is a doctoral candidate in counseling psychology at the University of St. Thomas, St. Paul, Minnesota.

About the Program

The activities in this guide were developed by the staff of the Amherst H. Wilder Foundation Community Assistance Program located in St. Paul, Minnesota. One of the largest such programs in the country, it serves more than six hundred clients each year and provides a comprehensive range of services: prevention, crisis intervention counseling, information and referral, advocacy, culturally specific programming, and assessments for women, men, teens, and children. The Wilder Men's Domestic Abuse Program is one of those services, and the activities and approaches described in this book are all used in that program.

The Wilder Men's Domestic Abuse Program was developed in 1981 in close cooperation with the county community corrections department and family courts. The program provides men with education and support to help them identify, reduce, and eliminate violent behaviors in their relationships. It uses a combination of therapeutic approaches to confront values, attitudes, and behaviors toward women and others, especially in the areas of violence, abuse, power, control, and manipulation.

The Wilder Men's Domestic Abuse Program has been featured in *Life*, in the Lee Grant documentary, *Battered*, and on the *Phil Donahue Show*. In addition, the staff have provided experiential training for professionals from around the United States, Canada, Germany, Guam, Iceland, and Puerto Rico.

Acknowledgments

There are many colleagues, coworkers, friends, victim/survivors, clients, and institutions who, in one form or another, have shaped this guidebook and workbook.

The Bigelow Foundation in St. Paul, Minnesota, provided a grant which allowed for the development of these books. Their invaluable support demonstrates their continued concern for violence and their willingness to address their concerns in a practical way. They are to be respected for their resolve and commitment.

Michael McGrane, Director of the Wilder Community Assistance Program (CAP), deserves special recognition. One of CAP's originators, Mike founded the Men's Domestic Abuse Program in 1981. He created many of the activities in this curriculum, and his group counseling expertise is highly visible throughout. He developed the House of Abuse model central to this curriculum and has used it when training professionals from around the world. Mike supervised the writing of these materials and provided his input along the way. His valuable contributions have increased the quality of the curriculum.

During the past two decades the counseling staff at CAP have worked tirelessly to help men examine and end their violence. The staff's commitment and daily work "in the trenches" have shaped the program's success. Their efforts, difficult and often unnoticed, are reflected in this manual. The CAP counseling staff have truly been the hope and inspiration that continue to motivate our work at ending violence in families and communities.

Certainly there has been a tremendous amount of support from the Amherst H. Wilder Foundation. I would like to thank Rodney Johnson, Director of Community Social Services; Claudia Dengler, Director of Services to Children and Families; and Thomas Kingston, President. They listened patiently to my ideas, concerns, and occasional whining, and have inspired me to see that the systems that serve women, children, and men can make changes. Kathy Tauer of CAP contributed tireless effort and countless hours throughout the years with her word-processing skills.

Rebecca Andrews and Vincent Hyman from the Wilder Publishing Center provided tremendous amounts of technical assistance. Becky got the project started and created a welcoming design, while Vince edited and revised to keep my writing lively and readable.

A critical component of the Wilder CAP model has been our successful collaboration with Ramsey County Community Corrections and Human Services. The dedicated efforts of the probation officers, family court workers, judges, supervisors, and child protection staff of Ramsey County have been key to providing effective violence intervention and prevention.

There are countless numbers of women's advocates and victim/survivors who have given their input and reviewed these materials both directly and indirectly. Their courageous efforts and profound experience have inspired us to continually scrutinize and improve our work with women, men, and children who live with violence.

I greatly appreciate the teachings I continue to receive from our clients. Their experiences, input, and feedback have helped improve the effectiveness of these activities for developing long-lasting change.

Finally, my personal support and inspiration in this process have been Teri Mathews, my wife, and Leah, my daughter. I could never say enough about how their continued love has helped me through the rough times.

David J. Mathews

Contents

Foundations for Violence-Free Living is a guidebook for counselors and others who work with, or plan to work with, men in heterosexual relationships who have abused a partner. It includes a collection of activities from our counseling experience with clients at the Wilder Community Assistance Program. Equally important, the guidebook describes the process we use and the special issues that typically arise in conducting each of these activities.

These activities and the issues they bring up are the core elements involved in helping a man—a group of men—begin to build a foundation for violence-free living. We discuss the underlying philosophy and goals of our program. We describe how we work with clients, including initial intake and individual counseling, some recommended policies, and special issues that come up in facilitating these groups. And we provide a set of activities, some of which are essential to our program, and others of which are optional, that you can draw on for your own program.

As you use this manual, please keep in mind the following points.

1. *Read the entire guidebook before using any activities.* The activities and information in this guidebook build on each other. You need to be familiar with the program's philosophy to best use the activities and to work with the special issues you encounter.

2. *This guidebook has two sections:*

    *   **How the Program Works**, describes the history, philosophy, and goals of this model, and how to best use the program. It provides some helpful ideas for conducting individual and group counseling and describes special issues related to domestic abuse group counseling processes with men.

    *   **Group Activities** contains twenty-nine activities, their accompanying worksheets, and guidelines for conducting each activity, as well as information about the kinds of issues you may encounter in each activity. Samples are included of all the worksheets.

3. *This guidebook is meant to be used with the accompanying participant's workbook.* The workbook, *On the Level: Foundations for Violence-Free Living*, consists of worksheets for the twenty-nine activities described in the guidebook. We suggest that you encourage the men to keep it with them throughout the program and afterwards. When complete, each man's workbook will serve as a record of his progress and a reference as he continues on the path to violence-free living.

4. *This guidebook is set up for ease of use and to help you continuously improve your efforts.* Each activity in the counselor's guidebook includes:

Goals
- The goals of the activity.

Required Worksheets
- A list of the worksheets required.

Format
- A description of how to conduct the activity.

Issues
- The important issues that the activity raises, both for the participants and the counselors.

Notes, Comments, and Observations
- Space to record your observations on the activity, so you can adapt and improve it in subsequent presentations.

Worksheets
- The actual worksheets the men will be using.

5. *This guidebook is* only *a guide.* Please feel free to experiment with and alter the activities as needed. Invent your own and add them to the book. Listen to your clients, your colleagues, and your gut, and let them be your guides. Remember as you work that each group of men is different; what works well with one group may fail with the next. While we have had great success with these activities, your counseling style, presentation, the group dynamics, and your relationships with the clients are the primary factors in being effective. We believe you will be most successful if you adopt an attitude of continuously learning, adapting, and improving both your presentation and the activities you use.

6. *For men with a pattern of violence, this program is only a beginning.* It will take a lifetime of effort for them to undo the patterns they have learned, as it will take generations for our society to forge nonviolent ways of life. Your work is part of a history-making movement. For centuries, partner abuse was considered acceptable—even a right—of men. Be patient with them and gentle with yourself in this process. You can't undo a culture of violence in sixteen weeks, but you can make a surprising amount of headway.

7. *As you use this guidebook, keep in mind that there are many aspects of running a men's domestic abuse program that we* don't *cover.* This guide does not tell you how to develop referral sources, how to set and administer fees, how to evaluate your program, how to market, how to conduct media relations, how to be a conscious and conscientious participant in the community, or how to influence public policy. All of these (and others not listed) are important aspects of running a good program. We assume that you have at least some of these components in place, or are working to develop them.

Our hope is that this guidebook will change and grow over time. We welcome your feedback and contributions. We are also available to train or consult with your staff. For questions or comments about any of these activities, contact us at:

Community Assistance Program
650 Marshall Avenue
St. Paul, Minnesota 55104
(612) 221-0048

Overview

The foundations for violence-free living in this guidebook represent years of work by grassroots efforts to end violence and abuse, a historical examination of these problems, and the practical experience of counselors at the Wilder Foundation. In 1981, the Wilder Foundation developed the early components of its domestic abuse program with the support and encouragement of the local county community corrections department. This was the beginning of an ongoing collaboration of efforts to meet the needs of families, children, women, and men who are survivors or perpetrators of violence in the family. These services are embedded in a larger network of Wilder Foundation services for distressed families and communities.

The model presented in this guidebook is a tested approach. It has been used with more than three thousand perpetrators of domestic violence. We are confident that the activities and approach presented in this guide will reduce the level of violence perpetrated by those who participate.

We believe our model is successful because of the following components:

1. *Our model is based on a combination of teamwork, relationships, and a philosophy that emphasizes accountability. Teamwork* is expressed through the support cofacilitators and other staff offer each other in this difficult work. *Relationships* between the facilitators and clients are based on openness, respect, and acceptance. And *accountability* is a key objective of all activities we do with the men, in which they learn about limits and taking responsibility for their behavior.

2. *We rely on group process.* The group holds each man accountable for his behavior. The men learn from each other and begin to see how they can support one another in making positive changes. The group process is essential to a counseling environment that combines respect, support, and confrontation. There are four overarching objectives in the group process:

   • All members of the system must be safe—partners, children, and participants.

   • Avoid overt or subtle collusion with the men's abusive attitudes.

   • Hold each man accountable for his behavior.

   • Increase each participant's understanding of how his behaviors have affected his family and others.

3. *We use and combine a variety of therapeutic approaches.* These approaches include: *cognitive/behavioral* (the restructuring of perception and emotion to change behavior); *psychodynamic* (understanding how the messages we have learned affect our current behavior); *empowerment* (each man must be responsible and accountable for his own actions); *reality therapy* (the use of confrontation to reveal what is really going on in a situation); and *educational* (a didactic presentation of material).

4. *We firmly believe that couples counseling is* not *effective, prudent, or appropriate when violence has been committed by a man in a heterosexual relationship.* A man who has been abusive must receive information, examine himself, and take responsibility for his behaviors before focusing on the relationship.

5. *We recognize that all members of the family system may ask for or need assistance in dealing with the man's violence.* (Note, however, that this guidebook only includes activities for the perpetrators of domestic violence.) In practice, we provide groups for survivors of abuse, including women, children, parents, and young adults. While not all agencies are able to offer these services, it is important that every agency know of and investigate local programs to which they can refer these people for support, advocacy, and other services.

6. *Our philosophy of abuse is comprised of eight principles.* We introduce these principles in the second activity, "Eight Program Principles," and discuss them at length in the description of that activity. The principles are:

   • Violence is a learned behavior. It has rewards and consequences.

   • Violence can be passed on from generation to generation.

   • Violence is reinforced by our society.

   • Violence can be unlearned. There are alternative ways to express feelings.

   • You are responsible for your own actions.

   • Provocation does not justify violence.

   • 100 percent rule: You are 100 percent responsible for your behavior in a relationship.

   • The only person you can control is yourself.

7. *We establish quality relationships and connections with other community services.* We are connected to a professional community, including women's shelters and children's programs, whose input helps us continually improve our program and keep in mind the needs of the

survivors of domestic violence as we work with perpetrators. Together, we participate on advisory boards, community initiatives, and workshops, and work closely on individual cases. In addition, our facility is located in or near to the communities we serve. We are within reach of other referral sources, families, and neighbors. These connections with our professional and geographic community are vital to maintaining a program that meets the needs of the community and the male participants—who, after all, come from and return to that community.

8. *We employ a flexible, diverse staff.* We feel our program succeeds in part because we select staff who are creative and open to new approaches, able to deal with the diverse cultural needs of participants and other staff, and willing to support each other. These characteristics are especially helpful in reducing staff burn out.

Using the Activities

There are twenty-nine activities in this guidebook. Some of these activities can be conducted in less than a single session of two to three hours. Others may take more than one session to conduct. We have organized the activities into six clusters: Essential Beginnings, Steps toward Insight, Becoming Accountable, Tools for Nonviolence, Personal Development, and Evaluations. These clusters help define the overarching purpose of the activities that comprise them, and their purpose is to help you select activities that will meet the needs of the clients you work with. Following are some guidelines on using the activities.

1. *We recommend at least sixteen sessions.* In this work, the most important consideration should be how much time a particular client requires to make the changes that will result in a life free of violence. But other pragmatic factors intervene: financial resources, the needs of the group, and your balance of therapeutic and educational interventions. There is no proven formula. However, we feel that at least sixteen sessions are needed to begin intervening with men who have abused a partner. Ideally, two to three years of some form of group work may be needed. We recommend the following fourteen activities as essential to laying the foundation for violence-free living:

   • Introduction to Group

   • Eight Program Principles

   • Men's Rules about Men

   • House of Abuse

   • The Pattern of Abuse

- Escalation Signals

- Responsibility Plan

- Most Violent Behavior

- Midterm Group Evaluation

- Personal Accountability Plan

- Self-Care

- Assertiveness

- Building and Maintaining a Support System

- Final Group Evaluation

2. *There is no magic in these activities.* In fact, your presentation, counseling style, and relationships with clients are the primary factors. Feel free to experiment with different ways of presenting the activities, shaping them to the needs of your clients and your personal style. Expand or shorten the time frames as needed. Keep in mind that one exercise may work well with one group and be unsuccessful with another. Choose additional activities from the six clusters that fit the particular needs of your clients. Use each presentation to structure future group sessions and learn from the group members how to best meet their needs.

3. *Work to achieve the best group size and setting.* We recommend a group of eight to ten men. As a practical matter, you may need to start with twelve to fifteen names on a list of potential participants; twelve may attend the first session, and through normal attrition, you'll end up with a group of ten. (Attrition has many roots: some men reoffend before entering the program and go to jail; some disappear; some change jobs. In our program, 70 to 75 percent of those who enroll complete the sixteen sessions. Don't be discouraged by attrition, but do study it to understand why it is occurring and what, if anything, you can do to affect it. Close contact with your referral sources helps slow attrition from the group.)

The group *setting* needs to be inviting and the chairs should be comfortable. Before the men attend the group, post some of the materials you'll be using—slogans, program principles, and so forth. You will need either a chalkboard or a writing easel, and enough markers, crayons, and extra pencils for the drawing and writing activities.

Intake and Individual Counseling

From the client's perspective, contact with the domestic abuse program begins with the first referral and ends after the completion of any after-care. (Even so, it may continue with any follow-up evaluation studies you are conducting.) Thus, we feel it is critical that all contacts be considered part of the continuum of intervention. While the focus of this guidebook is the actual group activities, we also see each man individually at intake and other counseling sessions. We offer the following suggestions for intake and individual counseling.

1. *Your professional relationship with a client starts with the first contact.* This is usually your first phone call to schedule an appointment. Be friendly and respectful and listen actively. Briefly state the purpose for meeting individually and a general schedule of any other sessions, including the group meeting times. Encourage questions or concerns from the client. This gives the client opportunity to observe you as you lay the foundation for security and understanding him. Your behavior models your expectations of the client.

   Explain your role in the agency and describe the group format. Discover something positive about the client and emphasize that others in the group may be able to gain from these attributes. Ask if he has had a prior group counseling experience and how this may help or hinder his participation in the new group setting.

   During this contact, you may encounter the first signs of resistance, as he may claim he doesn't have a problem, blame the system or his partner, state that he simply has an "anger problem," or offer some other excuse. Stay focused on your goal: schedule an appointment and give a general picture of the program.

2. *The first face-to-face contact is an opportunity to "hook" the client into receiving services.* You can do this in several ways, even as he displays resistance. Acknowledge that he probably would rather be elsewhere. Point out what other options he has (for many men, the only other option is jail). Express your desire that he make the best of his time in the group; ask for his participation, if only to help the time go faster. If he says that he's been through groups before or already "knows all this stuff," suggest that even though he may learn very little from the group, his experience will be of great help to the other men. Be clear with him that you know *you* can't change his behavior, and the information in the group will only be of help if he chooses to act on it; he can apply what's useful to him and disregard the rest.

Before he leaves your office, make a connection with this man. Show him that you are interested in his situation. Explain that you know he probably won't agree with everything you say, that you may challenge his beliefs and their origins, and that in the end, you both may agree to disagree.

Avoid getting drawn into an argument or power struggle with the client. It is normal to feel some anger or be disgusted by the actions he describes. However, you must remain focused on your goals: you are not interviewing him to decide *if* he should be in the group, but to evaluate *how* he will fit.

3. *Remember that the information you collect during individual sessions is strictly from the client's perspective.* At this time, the details of his situation or his taking total responsibility for his abusive behaviors are not as important as beginning to understand this man and developing goals for him. You can deal with his behavior, minimization, and denial during the group sessions. Don't try to deal with all of this in one individual session.

4. *Explain your program's requirements, policies, and requisite information releases.* For a description of suggested policies and releases see **Recommended Policies and Releases** on page 27.

   In general, you should explain all expectations, policies, and releases in the first intake session. Explain why each is necessary and the consequences of noncompliance. Make sure he understands, and encourage him to ask questions. If you don't know the answer to his questions, let him know that you will try to find the answer. For specific legal questions, consult with your agency's legal counsel.

   As formal as these releases seem, discussing them with the client is one way of building your relationship with him, and of uncovering and working with any resistance early on. For this reason, we feel the signing of releases and the intake process as a whole are an important part of our model.

5. *Discuss the group format and group process with the client.* Describe the group process and how it differs from informal men's groups. Explain that it's okay to talk about feelings and to disagree in group. Introduce some of the participation expectations. Discuss the importance of hearing everyone's opinion. Ask him what he hopes to gain from the group, and use his response to formulate the content and direction of some of the sessions. Explain that throughout the group process, you will want to know how he feels and what he needs from the group experience.

6. *Ask the client questions to learn more about who he is and his experience with violence.* Focus on his abusive and violent behaviors. Following are some questions you might ask:

- With whom have you been violent? Is this person living with you now? If not, what are the living arrangements?

- Describe the first time you were physically violent with your partner. How long had you been in the relationship?

- What incident brought you here?

- Describe the latest incident that has occurred.

- Describe what you feel was the worst violent incident in your relationship with your partner. What was happening before the situation? What did you do? What did she do? What happened afterwards?

- What issues have been difficult to discuss with your partner?

- What do you do when you get angry with people other than your partner? How do they know you are angry? Do you feel you have been abusive at times?

- What do you do when you get angry with your partner? How does she know you are angry? Do you feel that you have been abusive at times?

- What do you do when you get angry with yourself? What do you say to yourself?

- Have you ever tried to hurt yourself or thought of committing suicide? Have you ever attempted suicide?

- How would you describe your sexual relationship? How would your partner describe it? What conflicts do you and your partner have about sexuality and intimacy? What happens when one of you does not want to have sex?

- Have you ever tried to talk your partner into having sex when you knew she didn't want to?

- Tell me about your childhood. Where did you live, with whom did you grow up, how many brothers and sisters did you have? Did you live with anyone else for an extended period of time?

- Tell me about the violence you saw or experienced as a child. How did your parents discipline you as a child?

- Did you experience anything sexually inappropriate in your childhood? Were you ever molested? Has someone ever touched you in a private place and you felt uncomfortable?

- What alcohol and other drugs do you use now, how often, and how much? Describe your past alcohol and other drug use.

- Do you have any children? If so what are their names? Do they live with you? What is your relationship like with them?

- What effects have you observed in your children when violent incidents have occurred?

7. *Begin to reveal some of your philosophy of violence and abuse.* Share some of your goals for men in the group and some of the insights that you would like to see the client think about relative to your philosophy of abuse. Explain what you mean by "the only person you can control is yourself."

8. *Critical issues may arise during the individual sessions.* Issues such as childhood sexual abuse, suicidal thoughts, or mental health concerns may need to be addressed. Be prepared to provide referrals, information, and advocacy as needed.

9. *The individual sessions often provide a good opportunity for you to address specific issues related to resistant attitudes.* If you hear resistance, explore the client's feelings, and begin to establish a working relationship. This will save time and energy in group and ensure a healthier group process. (See **Working with Resistant Clients**, page 17, for more information.)

10. *Make it a priority to stay healthy personally and professionally.* Dealing with violence in relationships will affect you at all levels, but especially emotionally. Set up a support network with other professionals and use people outside of your workplace to maintain your balance. After sessions, make time for yourself.

Suggestions for Facilitating Groups

1. *Understand your own style and approach in doing group work.* Assess your strengths and limitations and balance them with the type of program you will be conducting. Decide whether you feel more comfortable in a teaching role or a counseling role. Use outside materials, staff, professionals, and supervision to develop your group facilitation skills. Continue to read about and investigate violence and group facilitation. Find new and creative ways to address issues related to domestic abuse. Use the "Notes, comments, and observations" section at the end of each activity to record ideas you can review for future groups and similar situations. We suggest that you develop a statement that spells out the psychological base or approach you use—the basic assumptions and principles of your group work.

2. *The relationship you have with a client will influence the group process.* Developing the relationship requires you to be an active, energetic participant in it. Be familiar with and mindful of the issues for the group and each member. Identify ways that each client can be helpful to the group. Maintain a respectful approach and avoid power struggles. Use interventions that are a balanced combination of confrontation and support.

3. *From the first session, develop goals for the group and individual members.* Keep in mind the following:

   • Clients' strengths, limitations, needs, and special issues.

   • Areas of resistance (or clients who may show more resistance) and the possible reasons for this resistance.

   • The group dynamic and ways to use the group process to help individual members.

   Reevaluate and alter these goals throughout the group process. High, unattainable expectations of clients may frustrate both you and the clients. Expectations of individual clients will vary; everyone does not have to be at the same level of understanding for you to move the group to the next topic. Some information will be of greater assistance to some group members than to others.

4. *Encourage the group members to provide information, feedback, confrontation, and supportive comments to each other whenever possible.* Most of what you say or ask should be directed toward the group. Avoid counseling individuals while in the group.

5. *Be an active listener.* You will be able to learn a great deal from your clients by being alert to common themes and underlying issues. Base your responses and interventions on what you hear. Direct these observations to the group often. Use reflective listening skills, paraphrasing what clients have just said and following up with a question to the group. (For example, "Bill feels confused when he's angry. Has anyone else ever felt that way?")

6. *Be aware of what is* not *being said.* Seating, body language, arriving late to the group, and avoiding discussion could be signals to you. Use this information by stating your observations to the group. Note which sessions or subjects trigger these behaviors, and be prepared to intervene. Use the group to help; for example, ask the group how they would feel if they were a particular man's partner and he communicated using the threatening body language he just showed in group.

7. *Provide information, support, and confrontation when needed.* Offer observations freely, even though they may seem critical of an individual's process or the group's process. Support the men by commenting on even

incremental progress. Helping the men surface their own insights is preferable to confrontation, but not always possible.

Some facilitators find confrontation difficult. Confrontation can be carried out in a variety of ways, including asking the group a question, asking for other members' opinions, and stating what you observe. Confrontation does not mean a power struggle; no one "wins" such a match.

On the other hand, some facilitators feel that confrontation is the only tool to use with men who have perpetrated abuse. In our experience, an ongoing confrontational style lowers the quality of service in several ways: the men raise their defenses higher and higher, they become less open to change, they feel they are being "beaten upon" by yet another authority, and they tend to respond with increasing resistance and possibly even aggression. Facilitators, too, can become exhausted with the ongoing effort of a confrontational style. In turn, this causes frustration and may decrease the potential for progress.

Balance confrontational approaches with supportive ones. Look for ways to give constructive input to group members, such as during process time. If you balance these approaches, the men will respect your directness and your support for them as human beings even if you disagree on some issues.

8. *Pay attention to the way you present yourself to the group.* Avoid long speeches, teaching, or preaching. Keep words and concepts as simple and concrete as possible. It may help to use examples or relate the experiences of other people. If members seem confused, rephrase your statements or ask another group member to explain your point. Don't be afraid of silence in the group setting. Too much teaching sets you up as the "person with all the answers," and also fosters a "group versus the counselor" atmosphere. Be aware of these dynamics as you develop your style of presentation.

9. *Allow the clients balanced freedom in the use of time while discussing topics.* Too much structure may obstruct some clients from sharing feelings and personal situations. Not enough structure will encourage clients to ramble, take too much time talking, or avoid talking about being abusive and taking responsibility for their behaviors. Other group members may be offended unless you can balance limits with some flexibility. Use group interventions such as cutting in and asking for someone else to respond to a question or asking the group how it feels when someone monopolizes the group's time. Point out group members who share time appropriately and encourage others to follow their lead.

10. *Regularly discuss the group process with the group.* Ask how it felt to do an activity after they have completed it. Ask about how easy or difficult it was. Let them criticize how you presented the material or handled a situation. Use this information to learn more about your counseling style and how you can improve the group process in the future

11. *In some activities, you may want to choose who speaks first.* This is especially beneficial if you give the person a lot of credit for what they have shared. There may be other times you want to ask for volunteers to begin a discussion. Use the silence that may occur as a time to decide who you will choose first in the next activity.

12. *Use motivated clients to lead the less motivated men by example.* Men who are motivated to complete the program are a benefit to the group process. Often they have already begun to have some insights into what they must change, and they have begun to see that their violent behavior is not acceptable. They have begun to recognize how hurtful their actions have been to their partners and other family members. They seem to be searching for ways to develop alternatives. They also tend to be more willing to experiment and try new things. Discourage abusive behavior by recognizing and encouraging men who are examining and addressing their violent behaviors.

13. *Be sure you discuss the group expectations, program principles, and concepts about domestic abuse early and often in the group process.* This way you can repeat and rephrase them throughout the sessions. Repetition helps group members understand the material, and lays the foundation for the interventions you will be making throughout the program.

14. *Be creative while doing group counseling.* Facilitating groups is an art, but one which you can learn. Draw from the experiences of others, but also build in the flexibility to try new exercises, interventions, and approaches. Try out different styles. Show your enthusiasm. Take your time, relax, and enjoy your group.

Cofacilitation

1. *We recommend a team of two facilitators, one male and one female.* We have conducted domestic abuse groups with many facilitator combinations, including one man as facilitator, one woman as facilitator, a man and woman in cofacilitation roles, two men cofacilitating, and two women cofacilitating. The male/female combination is an excellent

model for positive interaction and conflict resolution between men and women. While domestic abuse programs often employ primarily male counselors, there are many benefits to using female counselors in addition to male counselors. Many times, female counselors are able to identify and examine the men's violent behavior with more accuracy. The female perspective often helps group members better understand their partner's perspectives. When a female counselor facilitates the group, the men may more readily take responsibility for their behaviors. A woman in a position of authority can help the men develop a more respectful approach.

2. *Female facilitators note some differences (and challenges) in how they are treated by group members.* First, they reflect on the difficulty of listening to the overt, but mostly covert, negative attitudes these men have about women. Secondly, women facilitators tend to be treated—at best—as "one of the boys" or a different sort of woman, "not like the rest of them." When there is a male/female facilitator team, the clients are more likely to discount the female facilitator's comments. Group members are more likely to express their anger toward the woman facilitator, and they are more likely to direct their comments to the male facilitator even if the female facilitator asks the questions. Women facilitators are often asked to speak for "all women." These dynamics make cofacilitation more stressful for female facilitators, and *both* facilitators must keep this in mind as they work together.

3. *Cofacilitators must spend time together to become familiar with each other's styles, experiences, and philosophies.* Issues to explore together include:

- Who will lead the group initially, and how each facilitator envisions their roles changing over the course of the group sessions.

- Philosophy of abuse.

- Counseling styles, especially regarding confrontation.

- Expectations each facilitator has of the other facilitator. (Who will do the paperwork, who keeps case notes, who contacts referral sources, and so forth.)

- Handling mutual feedback and conflicts.

- Comfort levels with the issues that will be discussed.

- Attitudes toward women, men, the criminal justice system.

- How to deal with self-disclosure issues.

- How to deal with a client who is intoxicated, dismiss a man from the group, confront violations of group confidentiality, and so forth.

- Counselor boundaries in areas such as taking clients home, loaning money to clients, giving out home telephone numbers and addresses, befriending a client, and so forth. (We discourage these practices, but not all counselors do, so you will need to discuss them.)

Special Issues

Working with Resistant Clients

1. *Resistance to you, the program, and the information will be a common theme.* Approach resistant men as respectfully as you would any other clients. Be open to learning from them. In our experience, some of the men who are initially quite resistant make remarkable changes as the program progresses.

2. *Most clients are involuntary members of the group, while a few are voluntary.* A few men have been told to attend the group by their partners, and fewer still come of their own accord; these can be considered *voluntary* participants. Sometimes those men who voluntarily attend the group feel like outsiders, because they haven't had the recent court experiences of the majority of the men. (For this reason, some men who attend voluntarily may attempt to minimize their own behaviors by comparing themselves with those men who have been sent to the program involuntarily.)

   Usually, some outside agency or court order has given the clients few options besides attending the group. We refer to these clients as *involuntary* participants. Much of the resistance that the involuntary clients exhibit is addressed in this section. These men will pose some struggles at times for you.

   Regardless of how they come to the group, some men are able to see its benefits, especially those who have already had a positive counseling experience. Support their positive outlook and help them identify areas that they can focus on during the group sessions. Many times these clients may fit the "it's almost too good to be true" category. They seem motivated to learn and talk about their life problems. Capitalize on their openness to new information and use the individual sessions to better understand these clients. Ask them if you can have them talk about their viewpoints during group sessions.

3. *The individual sessions, if conducted prior to the start of the group, can be useful in addressing some of the resistant client's reluctance to attend group.* Areas to cover include their fears or concerns about attending

the group, what they would like to discuss in group, reassurance that they are not alone in their feelings and experiences, and some of the specifics of how the sessions will be conducted.

4. *The involuntary client tends to show a great deal of resistance during the beginning stages of the group process.* A client often feels relieved to simply tell you his side of the story, even if you directly disagree with him. Many of these men feel increasingly at ease as they find out that you will not put them down or refuse to listen to their version of what happened. This is a positive step toward building a relationship that will really assist the man to step out of his defensiveness. However, it is important that you let him know where you stand on what he says, even as you listen and acknowledge his version of the story.

5. *There are many ways resistance may be demonstrated.* To name a few:

   • Arriving late, refusing to attend, or refusing to participate.

   • Arguing with you or other members.

   • Questioning the group structure or content.

   • Accusing you or other members of having problems such as tardiness, not listening, not being truthful, and so forth.

   • Making negative comments.

   • Refusing to support other members.

   • Attempting to involve other members in negative ways.

   • Interrupting, refusing to listen to others, or trying to control the discussions.

   • Avoiding eye contact.

   • Nonparticipation in a seemingly passive manner.

6. *There may be other reasons for the above example behaviors.* Sometimes ethnic or cultural factors, reading problems, language differences, or the person's particular behavior style may look like resistance when it is not. Disagreements that look like resistance may be reasonable concerns that you need to respond to. Your counseling approach may be inappropriate for a particular client. Be open to and prepared for providing more appropriate resources to people with different needs.

7. *Address the underlying causes of resistance.* Resistance springs from feelings of anger, sadness, shame, guilt, fear, and so forth. Remember, the fact that they must see you and must attend the group is a constant reminder of their feelings and abusive behavior. The group process in itself causes a lot of stress for these men. Give them—and yourself—

time to let the resistance soften. Your relationship with each man and your consistency in the group process are key to reducing resistance. Focus on the positive aspects of the group and of each individual. Following is a list of techniques for reducing resistance.

- Point out the similar experiences and feelings of group members.

- Explain and clarify your expectations of the men.

- Accept disagreement and encourage discussion. Ultimately, you may have to agree to disagree.

- Allow some limited time for individuals and the group to vent their anger or frustration related to the "system," judges, or others.

- Clarify any questions about the judicial system and refer them to appropriate agencies or sources.

- Ask how the group can be more helpful.

- Direct open-ended questions to quieter members.

- Ask members with experience in certain areas to offer their views.

- Ask other members what they see happening and their observations of a resistant person's behavior.

- Hold a discussion about the resistant feelings of group members.

- Ask other group members to rephrase statements made by you or others.

- Encourage the men to openly express their feelings.

- Point out positive aspects or elements of what is said, even though the client was relating things in a negative or blaming manner.

8. *Pay attention to the effects of resistance on the group process.* When the resistance becomes destructive, respond to the behaviors. Make group interventions, give your observations, and avoid power struggles. The whole group is affected even if you direct your questions to one person.

9. *Be prepared for probing questions about you.* They may ask about your experience with domestic abuse, or the particular issue under discussion. Before starting a group, think through your possible responses. Some options include:

- Refusing to answer the question at this time.

- Exploring the reasons behind asking the questions.

- Answering in a general manner.

- Stating your experience.

Use careful judgment before disclosing personal information or experience to clients. They may be trying to avoid talking about their behaviors, they may feel insecure about sharing their own feelings, they may want to shift the entire focus of the group off of themselves, or they may have a genuine desire to know. Some helpful guidelines when answering personal questions are:

- Does my self-disclosure help the group or individuals understand the point I am trying to make?

- Have I resolved this issue for myself?

- Am I sharing this information for my benefit, or for the group's benefit?

- Anything I say about myself may be communicated back to me in a context different than what I had initially intended. Can this information be used against me in the future?

Special Situations

There are a variety of individual behaviors that affect the group dynamics. These include intoxication, sleeping during group, heavy denial and blaming, excessive complaining, refusing to participate, justification of abuse through culture or ethnicity, and abusive behavior in or outside of group. Following are some general guidelines for dealing with these behaviors in group:

- When a situation leaves you feeling stuck or unable to deal with a situation, try to buy time. Taking a break is always a good first course of action.

- Always consider the group dynamics when deciding how to intervene. Rely heavily on the relationships you have with clients when making interventions in the group process.

- As much as possible allow the group members to hold each other accountable for the group rules and expectations and for abusive behaviors. Facilitate this by asking questions of the group about a man's inappropriate behavior.

- Debrief tough group sessions with a cofacilitator, colleague, or another professional.

1. *Group member comes to group drunk or under the influence of other drugs.* When the situation is obvious, address the issue with the group immediately. (This is best done if you've already explained your policy on alcohol and other drug use at both the first face-to-face individual session *and* the first group session.) To intervene, you may choose to wait and see if one of the group members points out that the man is

under the influence; this way, the group takes charge of the problem. If no one points out the situation in a reasonable amount of time, try asking, "Does anybody notice what's going on with Jim here?" or "Who remembers the expectation we have about using drugs or drinking?"

Usually the policy is that no one is allowed to participate in group while under the influence of alcohol or other drugs. If the man resists leaving and tries to argue, first try repeatedly reminding the man of the group expectations from the first session. If this tactic doesn't get the man to leave, suggest that the group take a break, or that the group ask the man to leave. Before leaving, he should be reminded that his court worker will be notified about the situation. If the man is intoxicated, he cannot drive. Calling relatives, calling the police, or arranging for taxi service are all options. Remember, there is no point in arguing with a person impaired by alcohol or other drugs. Move quickly to a safe solution.

2. *Group member falls asleep in the group session.* It happens, despite your best attempts at being the fascinating facilitator you are. When it does, there are several options available to you.

    *   Wake the person up yourself.

    *   Signal (or ask) the person next to the sleeping man to wake him up.

    *   Allow the man to continue to sleep briefly as you begin to discuss the expectation that people stay awake in group.

    *   Offer the man an alternative such as standing up when he feels sleepy.

    Some of the interventions to use with the group may include asking:

    *   Does anyone remember the expectation about sleeping in this group?

    *   How does it affect the group when someone is sleeping?

    *   What message does this behavior send to the rest of the group? What does this behavior say about your respect for other group members?

    *   What needs to happen for you to stay awake in the group?

    *   What can other men do to help you stay awake?

    *   How can I assist you in staying awake?

    *   What should happen if this occurs again?

    *   Can sleeping be a way of avoiding the issues?

- Could this behavior be based on a lack of taking responsibility for your own behavior?

- Do you also tend to fall asleep at work, or is this behavior only happening here? Why don't you sleep at work? How is it you can control your sleeping in other situations more than here?

If the client habitually sleeps during group—even after you've intervened—explain some other consequences, such as contacting the court worker, removing the man from the group, or suggesting that he attend another program. State what you will do, and then follow through.

3. *A group member is into heavy denial and blame of others.* Initially, many of the men enter the program with this attitude. Defensiveness and blame are mechanisms by which these men avoid focusing on their personal issues of power and control. Some of the clients will be blatant with their denial and blame of others while other clients will be quite covert. These attitudes and behaviors stem from the feelings of guilt and shame that permeate the resistance. (See **Working with Resistant Clients**, page 17.)

When blame and denial occur in the group setting, the first step is to stay calm. Don't react to the statements in a way that is blaming or creates a further power struggle. Ask questions related to the situation the man is describing. Use the time to better understand his point of view. Have him focus on his feelings about and reactions to the people he is blaming. Ask other group members if it sounds like this person is taking responsibility for his behaviors. Emphasize that the only person he can control is himself. Have him identify the impact of his blaming on others—might they be scared, confused, or hurt by what he says?

Typically, a number of men join in to support blaming comments, especially early in the group sessions. It may help to allow a specific amount of time for just dumping these feelings. When they have completed their allotted time (without you saying much if anything at all) ask them to discuss how it felt to talk about and listen to the blaming. Then suggest that they could spend the entire group time just expressing themselves the way they were, or they could focus on people they have total control over—themselves. Point out that this latter focus will have more positive effects for each of them than continuing to blame others, which only results in frustration. Ask them to recommit to the process, to make the best out of the situation and their time, and to recall the goals of the group.

Sometimes denial and blame resurface in the later stages of the group process. This is natural; as time goes by, the clients feel safe expressing their true feelings about what you have said, including statements you made five or ten sessions in the past. This phenomenon is an indicator of their deep-seated attitudes about abuse and violence, not a sign that you are an ineffective facilitator. Remember that it will take more than the few months you have with these men to change their thinking.

4. *A group member complains at length about the system.* Many men in domestic abuse groups find it easy to project their anger, frustration, hurt, and shame on the courts or other systems. If these concerns are raised early in the group process, it may be appropriate to allot a specific time for the men to vent their complaints. Use the same tactic for this as you used with their expressions of denial and blame. After they vent, explore their feelings and thoughts about their real opportunities to change the system in the short term. Point out that in the present, all they can really control and change is themselves.

   It may be helpful to ask the group members to name specific people in the system who treat them unfairly. The more you can get them to personalize the "system," the more difficult it becomes to complain about it. When they talk about who they are angry with, they often seem to be able to understand the position the judge (or police officer, or whoever they identify) is in when responding to domestic abuse cases.

5. *A group member becomes abusive toward another member, a cofacilitator, or you.* Earlier, we noted that one of the objectives of this program is that *all* members in the program must be safe. Therefore, begin addressing this problem before it occurs with good preventive strategies. In addition to the discussion of group expectations during the first few sessions, prevention strategies might include asking the group to think through or role-play what to do should one member become abusive toward another or toward a facilitator. Furthermore, you and your cofacilitator should discuss how you will handle such a situation. When will you call for a break in the group? Under what conditions would you call the police? How will you signal each other that some action needs to be taken? In all cases, avoid taking lightly any sort of abuse or possible intimidating language or behavior.

   When a group member becomes abusive toward another group member, it's important that the facilitator not get in the middle of the fight. Encourage the men to work it out with words. As soon as you detect tension, consider asking all the men who are *not* involved in the tension to talk about what they are sensing and observing. If need be, take a break. Let the other men get some coffee or use the rest room. Give each man involved in the conflict the opportunity to de-escalate before starting to talk about the situation.

When a group member becomes abusive toward a cofacilitator, quickly assess the situation and make eye contact with the cofacilitator. Use direct, immediate interventions with the abusive individual, and begin to distract his focus. For example, you might state "What you said is offensive and intimidating; what are you feeling right now? How does the group perceive what this man is saying?" After some discussion, you and your cofacilitator might give the group a brief break during which you can review your options. When you reconvene the group, spend more time discussing the situation with the group. Ask how they felt about the situation, what they noticed about everyone's behavior, and what will help them feel safe in the group again. Use the situation to let the men hear the cofacilitator's feelings; this will help the men understand some of the effects of abuse. After the group, you and the cofacilitator should discuss how the situation went and plan for future such events.

When a group member becomes abusive toward you, follow the plan you've mapped out with your supervisor, colleagues, or cofacilitator if you have one. Avoid getting trapped by the idea that you need to make final decisions at any point during the situation. Look for ways to buy time. At some point, either with the man in the room or with the other group members, the abusive behavior needs to be identified as abuse and discussed with the group. In particular, explain how you felt in order to emphasize how the victim of abuse feels. Guide the group through their initial denial or minimization of how you felt. Remember, though, that the group is not there to take care of you; let them know this and that you will be talking with your colleagues and peers about the situation.

6. *A group member refuses to participate.* When a group member refuses to participate, think about how you can involve the group in making the man accountable. Ask the other group members their perspective on the man's participation for the past few weeks. Try to find something positive in their statements; for example, they may refer to having spoken with him during break, and that is a form of group participation. In addition to searching for positives, ask group members what it feels like to have this person slow the process down, try to escape participation, distract the group, or ask other people to make decisions for him. Ask the man directly what feelings or other factors keep him from participating in the group.

You can also address nonparticipation indirectly. Ask the group to suggest consequences for hypothetical situations. For example, ask "what would happen to a man who does not complete this program and is sent back to his probation officer or court worker?" At some point you may need to define clearly what is acceptable participation and what constitutes nonparticipation.

7. *A group member denies ever being abusive in his life toward anyone.* Review the definition of abuse with this man and the other group members. There may be a point at which you will need to be satisfied with this man simply stating that he has been verbally abusive. However, if he admits this much, then you can also connect the verbal abuse to emotional and other types of abuse. He may maintain that even though you see his behavior as abusive, he does not define his behavior in this manner. Point out the likelihood that he will be violent in the future so long as he continues to deny or minimize how his behaviors have affected others. Explain your disagreement with his position.

   The observations and peer pressure of the other group members may be your best first course of action. Ask them how this man's behavior might look to his partner or children; ask how it feels when one group member withholds information when the rest of the group has talked openly; or ask their opinions about whether this particular man has ever been abusive.

   For more discussion on dealing with this type of client, see the **Issues** section of the activity, "Most Violent Behavior" page 84.

8. *A man uses race, culture, or ethnic background as a justification for being abusive.* Ask this man to clarify the specific ways culture is responsible for his behavior. Ask the other group members how this man's explanations sound. Another approach is to ask the group to reframe and restate his explanations. Regardless of his explanations, your bottom line must be that while this man is conveying an opinion, it does not agree with yours; no one deserves to be hurt or abused.

   Often men use culture to justify the right to spank or hit a child. Challenge their ideas about their own cultures. Ask, "Does any culture value the hurting of one human being by another human? Are there cultures that do not encourage or support striking children? How have these cultures (or countries) been successful?"

9. *A client's partner contacts you.* Always consult your agency policy and the state or local laws that govern the release of information. If you have a signed release of information by the man, you may speak openly with his partner; if not, you may need to speak only in hypothetical terms. Find out why she is contacting you and what she expects you to do as a result. Inquire about her safety. Suggest she develop—or help her develop—a plan to keep herself and her children safe if there is any risk of further abuse. Provide referrals to local shelters or advocacy groups when appropriate.

Counseling Diverse Groups of Men

Many domestic abuse programs serve clients with a diverse mix of ethnic, cultural, racial, and class backgrounds. As a counselor and group facilitator, you need to be comfortable working with all types of people. You must become culturally competent—that is, you must be aware of and attend to the diverse backgrounds in each group of men. Following are some suggestions for improving your cultural competence.

1. *Examine your own perspective and fears about differences in race and class.* Talk this over with colleagues in your program, as well as those from other agencies. Attend workshops and other programs that help you explore and change your own biases.

2. *Be up front about the diversity within the group.* Admit from the beginning that there are differences among the men in the group, and point out some of these differences. Discuss where people were born, and with which culture(s) they identify. Explain that everyone can learn from each other's experiences. Avoiding the issue only sends the message that you are reluctant to deal with it. Thus, men who are concerned about this may interpret your behavior as being naive or even racist.

3. *Admit your own limitations and biases to the group.* Let them know that part of your job is to encourage everyone to state their opinions as well as their expertise about their own culture. Explain that you are continuing to learn about your own biases and are working to change them.

4. *By directly addressing the issues raised by group diversity, you will contribute to the accessibility and respectful nature of the group process.* This examination and openness also contributes to a feeling of safety for those men who routinely experience prejudice and oppression. These men, in particular, may feel from the first group meeting that they will be avoided or discounted, just as they have been in the past.

5. *Help the men recognize the parallels between racism, sexism, and violence against women.* You can start a brisk discussion by suggesting that group members who have experienced oppression may be able to empathize more closely with the oppression of women. In the course of this discussion, it may be appropriate to ask these men about their personal experience dealing with oppression, and then draw the connection between the reactions and feelings of women as they deal with men.

Recommended Policies and Releases

While every program has its own unique policies and information releases, there are some situations that arise for every program. There are also local and state regulations and state professional codes of conduct that influence policies. We recommend you develop policies or releases to deal with the following issues.

1. *Nonparticipation in group.* There are many instances when men with resistant attitudes refuse to actively participate in group. You need to think through your response ahead of time. We suggest that you design a policy that allows the facilitator to dismiss a man who is not participating after several documented attempts to get him to participate. Some agencies have guidelines that services cannot be refused except in potentially dangerous situations. In this case, the policy could be to put the man on notice that he will not be signed off as having completed the program until he has fully participated in the remaining activities. Regardless of the policy, it is always prudent to buy some time and consult with your colleagues before making a final decision.

2. *Client rights and responsibilities.* We ask each client to read and sign a sheet explaining his rights as a client and what we expect of him. These include the right to:

   • Respectful and courteous service.

   • Information on his assessment, recommended counseling, and estimated length of treatment.

   • Explanations of all releases, requirements, and fees.

   • Refuse treatment or choose to receive counseling elsewhere, within the limits imposed by insurance coverage or court order.

   • Information about other services available in the community.

   • Coordinated transfers to other service providers if needed.

   • Advance notice of changes in service or fees.

   • Assert these rights without retaliation.

   • Discuss with the counselor his or her training.

Some of the client's responsibilities include the responsibility to:

   • Be respectful of staff and others.

   • Be on time or call in advance to reschedule.

- Not come for services under the influence of alcohol or other mood-altering substance.

- Follow smoking ordinances.

- Dress appropriately.

- Pay fees.

3. *Data privacy and confidentiality*. This is a crucial area for these men, as many of them are already involved in the court system. In most states, mandatory reporting laws allow certain records to be subpoenaed. We recommend that you:

   - Discuss who you must inform and what you must do should you hear about child abuse or neglect or if you believe he is going to hurt himself or someone else. Explain any state or local laws.

   - Explain how you communicate with court officials and to what extent you share information. Be sure your information releases clearly explain the nature of your contact with officials and what information is usually exchanged.

   - Explain how the program responds to court subpoenas ordering the program to hand over case notes or information regarding the client.

   - If you are doing any research related to the information that clients give you, ask their permission and explain the nature, use, and availability of the research to others.

   - Explain what information will be available to the client from your records, whether you will be writing any summary reports, and to whom you will send these reports.

4. *Releases of information*. Information releases are needed for a variety of contacts: with court workers and ex-partners, to allow video or audiotaping of group sessions, and for other purposes. At intake or individual counseling sessions, explain when these are needed and when they are not needed for you to share information. In particular:

   - Discuss who you need releases from—for example, the client's partner, ex-partners, psychiatrists, psychologists, other social workers, doctors, school personnel, and other programs he is participating in.

   - If you use audio or videotapes of the group, explain how these recordings are used and for what purposes; for example, whether the tapes are used for supervision and training of the counselors, external training of professionals, or for members who cannot read or write. Explain how and when tapes are erased.

Sometimes a man refuses to sign one or more releases. Some agencies state strongly that refusal to sign a release for a facilitator to contact a partner (or ex-partner) is cause for not allowing the man to participate in the program, while other agencies have no paperwork in this area at all. We emphasize that releases be signed in order for a man to participate. However, we avoid power struggles whenever possible. Most of the men expect to hear "sign this release or else." In our experience, a man is most likely to sign a release when the counselor has established a relationship with him, and when the counselor explains what the release is for, who will make the contact with the partner, and why such contact will be made. When a man is hesitant about signing a release, we let the man know that signing the release is an expectation of the program, but give him a day or more to consider signing it. Power struggles are unproductive, especially early in the counselor-client relationship. Should he continue to refuse, we suggest a meeting with his court worker and explain that he will have to discuss the fact that his decision not to sign a release may prevent him from being accepted into the program.

5. *Use of alcohol and other mood-altering drugs.* We strongly recommend that you develop a policy that prohibits attending the group while under the influence of alcohol or other mood-altering drugs. Explain this policy to each client and ask if he feels he can abide by this expectation. Explain that attendance in group while under the influence of chemicals prevents him from learning and distracts other men. Point out that there may be men in the group who are struggling with sobriety. Explain the consequences for this behavior and that the final determination of his condition will be in your hands. The consequence we usually use is to ask a man who is using chemicals to leave the group and contact his counselor the next day to talk about what he must do to reenter the group. We also ask the man to contact his court worker, whom we call to confirm the contact.

6. *Firearms in the home.* We recommend that you develop a policy asking that the men remove any firearms from the home. In our experience, a rifle or handgun which is easily accessible is more likely to be used— either to hurt or to intimidate. While enforcement of this policy is difficult, state your concerns emphatically.

7. *Living with a partner he has abused.* We suggest that the man live separate from his partner for the first two months of group. Too often, the initial steps of the program create a false sense of safety. The two-month period gives him a minimal amount of time to begin to focus on his own issues and look at ways of taking care of himself. As with the firearms policy, there is little you can do but suggest this living arrangement. If he has a court order keeping him away from the

household for an extended period, we insist that he follow the court order, and we report any violation that we hear about.

Men who have abused their partners can and will change given the opportunity, support, and challenge to do so. The techniques and policies we've suggested here, as well as the activities that follow, are one path to that change, but by no means the only path. They have proven effective for many of the men we work with in St. Paul, Minnesota, as well as at other locations across the United States. We hope that you will use and adapt this guide to fit with the men you work with and the communities where you practice.

Good luck in this difficult but essential work.

Cluster

Essential Beginnings

Introduction to Group

Goals

In this activity, participants will:

1. Understand the purpose and nature of the Men's Domestic Abuse Program.

2. Begin to feel less isolated as men who have been abusive.

3. Become comfortable in the group setting.

4. Develop, as a group, expectations for behavior within the group.

5. Develop, as a group, goals for what members want to learn and discuss.

6. Begin to talk with other men who have been abusive.

Required Worksheet

Getting to Know Other Group Members (Worksheet 1)

Format

Begin by welcoming the men to the group. Use this time to further your relationship with the group as a whole. Include some of the following points:

- "Congratulations for coming. This is the first step, and the first session is usually the most difficult."

- "You had a choice to come or not and you chose to come. Many men choose not to come."

- "I don't want this time to be viewed as a punishment, but as a help."

- "I would guess there are a few men who don't think they need to be here, and who feel they have better things to do. Let's try to make the best of this time."

- "The main focus of the group will be on men's abusive and violent behaviors."

- "This is your group. I am the facilitator and not a group member. I have other places to go with my issues."

- "Many of you have already sized each other up and tried to figure out how you are different from these other men. I believe you will discover that we are all much more alike than different. We will listen for and emphasize those similarities in this group."

- "This is a unique setting for most of you. We will talk about personal issues, specifically violence, on a level deeper than many of you have talked in the past. We will focus on taking responsibility for our behaviors, talking about nonviolent alternatives, learning to express feelings appropriately, and learning to take care of ourselves."

- "In this group, you will be able to deal with problems and get ideas from other men in a way that's different from what you may receive from sources outside of this group. This type of group and of sharing at emotional levels is not easy for men. It goes against what our culture has taught us about how men should act."

- "There are no guarantees and no magic cures to domestic violence. Dealing with your own violent and abusive behavior is a long process. Going through this group may not put your relationship back together or even prevent you from being abusive in the future. Hopefully it can offer you some tools to use and remember long after you've left the group."

- "You owe yourself a lot of credit for being here. It takes a lot of courage to walk in this door and face things that are uncomfortable, even painful. Change is difficult, but it must be your decision to change. No one can change for you."

- "I do not have all the answers. That is why a group setting is so much better to address these issues. You will learn a lot more from the other men than from me."

Next, introduce yourself (and cofacilitator, if there is one), volunteering only pertinent information you feel will help the group.

Ask each man to introduce himself using his first name. After everyone has done this, repeat the process but reverse the order. Then ask a group member if he can name everyone. If he forgets a man's name, have him ask that man. You may also want to check the climate of the group by suggesting that each man says his first name followed by one feeling about attending the group.

There are many variations to this introduction process, depending on your goals for the exercise and the amount of time. For example, ask the first person to your right to begin by saying his name. The person to his right will say his own name plus the name of the first person to speak. This continues around the room until the last man must name everyone in the group.

Explain the basic format of the group. Points to include are:

- Length of each session and the number of weeks the program will run.

- Attendance requirements and any policies regarding absence.

- When breaks will be held.

- Basic format for each session: presentation, discussion, personal sharing, and group support.

- A great deal of the benefit from the group comes from the members' ideas, challenges, and mutual support.

- "You may not agree with everything that is presented or said. Let the counselors and group know your opinion. Ultimately we may need to agree to disagree."

Ask the group what expectations they have of each other, and then ask what they expect from you as a counselor. Finally, let them know what you expect from them during the sessions. Use this time to emphasize any policies, explain the reporting laws for your state, discuss court conditions, and explain the program requirements. Most of these expectations will be a repetition of what you have told the men in the individual sessions.

As group members generate ideas in response to these questions, one counselor (or a group member) writes the ideas on the board while the other counselor (or another group member) writes them on paper. Copy these and distribute them during the break or the next group session.

Some expectations that should be included and discussed are:

- *Attendance*. Discuss the importance of regular attendance. State the attendance requirement policy. Ask members to call ahead if they cannot attend.

- *Punctuality*. Note that the group will start on time, and frequent latecomers disrupt the group process. State the program late policy or have the group develop their own. (For example, if someone knows he'll be more than ten minutes late, he should not come to group.)

- *Confidentiality*. Explain that what is said in group, stays in group. Members can tell people outside the group what they are learning, but not details about anyone else in the group.

- *Exceptions to confidentiality for counselors*. These include:

  Safety of Self and Others—The counselor will need to break confidentiality if a client talks about hurting himself or someone else.

  Child Protection—In most states, counselors are required by law to report suspected child abuse or neglect to Child Protection Services.

Court Workers—Counselors will notify the court worker if a group member reports becoming violent or is arrested.

Court Subpoena—Both written records and counselors can be subpoenaed to court.

- *Counselor boundaries.* Discuss your professional (or required) boundaries should you encounter a group member outside the group setting, such as at a social gathering or while shopping. (We suggest that you let the client take the lead; if he greets you, respond. Lengthy conversations about the group or yourself may be inappropriate.)

- *Respect for others.* Ask group members to allow others to form their own conclusions; to avoid "shoulds"; to give input respectfully; and to avoid verbal, physical, or emotional abuse of each other and the counselors. Explain that the best way for them to refer to their wife, partner, or girlfriend is to use her first name. Ask the men to avoid labels or derogatory names. Emphasize being respectful to those people not present as well as to the men in the group.

- *No eating or smoking in group.* These behaviors distract other members.

- *No alcohol or other drug use.* Explain your program's alcohol and other drug use policy. For example, members who drink alcohol or use drugs the day of group will not be allowed into the group, or will be asked to leave.

- *Challenge each other.* Explain that you expect the men to challenge each other's violent behaviors, hold each other accountable for the group expectations, and support each other's decisions to act in nonabusive ways. Emphasize the importance of respecting each other's views.

After discussing group expectations, ask the men what their goals are—what they want to learn, discuss, or understand about violence or abuse. As with group expectations, one counselor writes these ideas on the board, while the other (or a volunteer from the group) writes them on paper. Copy these and hand them out during break or at the next session.

Explain that during the course of the sessions members will get to know each other. To begin this process have the men pair up and ask each other for the following information:

- First name.

- Who they abused.

- One thing they want to get out of the group.

- A personal strength.

Have them fill in this information on the worksheet, Getting to Know Other Group Members (Worksheet 1). Allow no more than five minutes to exchange this information. Then have group members repeat the process with someone else. Finally, have them pair up with a third person during break and repeat the process a third time. When they return from break, ask them to share what they learned from their partner. If they forgot, or did not get the information, have them ask that person at that time within the group.

After every man has spoken, ask the group if they heard any similar themes in the information. Capitalize and focus on similarities of situations, feelings, or thoughts.

To close the first activity, let the men know that you appreciate the effort it took for them to come to this first group. Explain that beginning with the next session, you will be asking for volunteers to "take time." This will be their opportunity to discuss current personal problems, abusive incidents, or daily life concerns and to receive comments and support from the group. Explain that you expect that they honestly and openly tell the group about any current abusive behavior, because acknowledging such behaviors is a first step toward change. Finally, point out that it is also important for them to talk about the *positive* things that are happening in their lives.

Encourage members to call you if problems arise during the week and they need feedback or support.

Tell the men that you will start a phone list so they can call each other for support. Explain that they do not need to give their phone numbers if they choose not to.

Before closing, ask each member for a one-word description of how he feels now compared to when he started the session. Then ask each man to state a strength about who he is as a person. (He may use the same strength he shared earlier.) Ask for a show of hands from those who plan on returning for the next session.

Thank the members for coming to group.

Issues

1. *There is usually considerable tension during the first group.* Clients do not know each other, and some have never been in a group. Most feel unsure of themselves and ashamed of being seen in the group. You also may be apprehensive and unsure of how these men will mix, but it is up to you to set a positive mood. It may help to state your anxiety or ask the group members to do so. Remember, you are not responsible for the group's behavior. Your responsibility is to facilitate a safe and respect-

ful environment that promotes positive change. Challenge and confront, yet avoid no-win power struggles. Appropriate humor helps relieve the tension.

2. *Each individual has unique issues and concerns.* These differences are important and should be acknowledged. But it is also critical to point out similarities, as these create a sense of belonging and help build cohesiveness. Revealing similarities breaks down obstacles of isolation, feelings of shame, and resistance to the group.

3. *Resistance from group members may be demonstrated in many different ways during this first session.* See **Working with Resistant Clients**, page 17.

4. *Remember, you do not have to tell everything in the first group session.* Take your time. You will have many opportunities to make your points and emphasize certain material throughout the sessions.

5. *Be flexible in allowing group discussion on certain points.* Provide ample time for questions about what you have said or any decisions the group has made. Assure them that you do not have all the answers, but will try to find answers for any unanswered questions.

6. *Within the first few sessions there is a tendency for group members to want to focus their discussion on blaming others.* See "A group member is into heavy denial and blame of others," page 22.

7. *You may have time during the first session to move on to a presentation of the Eight Program Principles.* Sometimes, the men are not very talkative during the first session. Move on to the discussion of the principles if there's time, but please don't rush your presentation.

Notes, comments, and observations:

Participant's Workbook Sample

Goals

In this activity, you will:

1. Understand the purpose and nature of this program.

2. Begin to feel less isolated as a man who has been abusive.

3. Become comfortable in the group setting.

4. Develop, as a group, expectations for behavior within the group.

5. Develop, as a group, goals for what members want to learn and discuss.

6. Begin to talk with other men who have been abusive.

WORKSHEET 1   Getting to Know Other Group Members

1. His first name:_____
   - Who the abuse was against: _____
   - One thing he wants to get out of the group meetings: _____
   - A personal strength: _____

2. His first name:_____
   - Who the abuse was against: _____
   - One thing he wants to get out of the group meetings: _____
   - A personal strength: _____

3. His first name:_____
   - Who the abuse was against: _____
   - One thing he wants to get out of the group meetings: _____
   - A personal strength: _____

May Not Be Reproduced

Goals

In this activity, participants will:

1. Learn and understand the program's philosophical basis.

2. Discuss whether they agree with the eight principles that constitute the program's philosophy.

3. Increase their personal interactions within the group.

4. Begin to develop their own philosophy of violence and abuse.

Required Worksheets

Eight Program Principles (Worksheet 2)
My Philosophy of Abuse and Violence (Worksheet 3)

Format

Open this session with a discussion of the eight program principles that underlie the approach of this program. These principles are:

1. Violence is a learned behavior. It has rewards and consequences.

2. Violence can be passed on from generation to generation.

3. Violence is reinforced by our society.

4. Violence can be unlearned. There are alternative ways to express feelings.

5. You are responsible for your own actions.

6. Provocation does not justify violence.

7. 100 percent rule: You are 100 percent responsible for your behavior in a relationship.

8. The only person you can control is yourself.

Write the first principle on the chalkboard. Under it, write "For" on one side of the chalkboard and "Against" on the other side of the chalkboard. Divide the group in half and have the group on the "For" side argue in support of the principle. The other group will argue against the principle. Monitor their discussion, changing sides to provide arguments for each group.

After five to ten minutes of discussion, write the next principle on the board and switch the two groups' perspectives on the argument. (The "Fors" are now "Againsts" and vice versa.) Repeat this process until all eight principles have been discussed.

When this activity is completed, have the men discuss these points from their personal perspectives. Ask how it felt to defend the side opposite their views. Discuss how it felt to talk about these principles with a group of men.

Now ask the men to turn to the Eight Program Principles worksheet. Explain that these are the eight principles of the program. Discuss each principle from your perspective. Have the men answer the questions under each principle. Discuss their responses at length. Encourage them to identify and state whether they agree or disagree with each principle.

Explain that the eight principles will be woven throughout future sessions. Let them know *your* bottom-line stance on abuse: Violence is never an acceptable way to solve problems with a partner. Encourage questions and comments. As you clarify and explain the principles, have them record some of the following thoughts on their worksheets:

1. *How do we learn to be violent? In other words, what are the rewards and consequences of violence?*

   Violence has rewards and consequences. Many men have not thought about the rewards for violence. Have them talk about how violence helps them release tension, energy, or stress; get their own way; control others; gain a powerful reputation with peers; or prove their masculinity.

   The negative consequences of violence include going to jail; hurting oneself, someone else, or a loved one; scaring people, or making someone we care about fear us; losing a relationship and children; and other losses, such as employment, housing, and so forth.

   If there were no rewards and only negative consequences for violence, chances are good there would be no violence. Men who choose violence downplay (minimize) its negative consequences and focus on its rewards.

2. *How does society reinforce violence?*

   Violence and abuse are reinforced as solutions to problems in music, media, television shows, commercials, advertisements, and magazines. We sometimes see forceful manipulation used as a tool in the political world, by authorities such as the police, politicians, and employers, in sports, in religion, in school, by our peers, and by parents.

   No single one of these messages has shaped our view of violence, but the constant bombardment and compounding of these messages affect our view.

3. *How can violence be passed through generations?*

   Violence is not contained in one's genes—it is not a basic element of humanity. We learn violence from growing up around it or with it. We often learn violence from our parents, but we can pick it up from other sources as well: peers, school, teachers, siblings, neighbors, other adults, the military, and so forth. This is why we say violence can be passed on. We can also decide to stop it in our own lives so that we won't transfer the learning to others.

4. *How can violence be unlearned?*

   Discuss and list some alternatives to violence. Practicing these alternatives is essential to changing behavior—to "unlearning" violence. In addition, we can unlearn violence by examining our attitudes, changing our self-talk, counteracting violent messages, and counteracting the negative messages we receive and believe about ourselves. Finally, we can help others unlearn violence by being a good model for children and other adults: by our behavior, we can show that violence can be unlearned.

5. *In what ways is a man responsible for his own behavior?*

   This question can best be answered by asking some other questions: If we are not responsible for our own behavior, then who is? If we drive while drunk or high, cause an accident in front of many witnesses, but can't remember a thing, who is at fault?

6. *Can't someone provoke you into violent behavior? Does provocation justify violence?*

   No matter how many times a person "pushes your buttons," it is not okay to react violently. Questions of self-defense may come up here; acknowledge the existence of self-defense, but point out that self-defense is rarely the case for a man in a domestic assault. Ask the men to honestly examine the difference between these issues. Be prepared to express your own opinion during the discussion. Men want to hear that it is okay to act violently; they tend to invent almost impossible scenarios in which violence against a partner is justified. Rather than creating a power struggle by calling the scenario ridiculous, diffuse these questions by turning them back to the group: What would you do? How can one avoid being in a situation like this?

7. *Who is responsible for a man's behavior in the relationship?*

   Each person is 100% responsible for his or her side of the relationship. This contradicts common phrases such as "relationships are 50/50," "it's a two-way street," and "it takes two to tango." Men can let go of trying to be responsible for their partner; they can also let go of the expectation that a man's partner is responsible for his behavior or somehow "makes him do things." Men resist this principle. Explain that we all need to be responsible for our own behavior, particularly when we are in a relationship.

8. *Can a man really control anyone besides himself?*

   Discuss who the men think they can control or have wanted to control in their lives. Explore their beliefs when they say they *do* control someone else. Examine their reasons for wanting to control someone else; what are the rewards and negative consequences for trying to control someone?

For an increased emphasis on these principles, ask the men to turn to the worksheet, My Philosophy of Abuse and Violence. Tell the men to complete this sheet from their point of view, now that you have had the above discussions. Explain that they will discuss their responses in a follow-up session. Encourage honesty in their responses, even if their answers differ from the eight principles. During a follow-up session, discuss their responses and reasons for their views.

Issues

1. *Be prepared for a great deal of resistance.* The men may resist arguing from a point of view opposite from their own. Make this a fun exercise by encouraging them to use their acting abilities. If some men resist participation, have the two groups meet separately to plan their arguments. This removes the pressure to perform from individuals who don't like to participate.

2. *Make sure that you think through these eight principles and talk them over with others to strengthen your ability to communicate them.* Consider your responses to some of the following questions: "What about self-defense? What if I was cornered by someone with a gun and a knife? Aren't all of these principles too ideal to live by? Isn't that just the way life is? What can a man do, since the system is all screwed up? Were these principles written by women? Is violence always wrong? When is it okay to be violent? Relationships are a two-way street, and it takes two to tango, doesn't it? Can I be violent if my family is in danger? What would you do if someone had a gun on you and all you could do was hit him? Have you (the counselor) ever been violent?"

3. *If you have a cofacilitator, make it a priority to discuss these principles at length before the first session.* If you do not agree with each other you must be aware of each other's views and perspectives on these principles. Review the list of questions above. Let each other know how you may respond.

4. *The eight principles are not magic.* They are just a beginning. If you can develop more, do so.

5. *A man's statement that he agrees with all eight principles is not an indicator that he has completed the program.* In fact, if men do not resist these principles at this early stage, you can be fairly certain that their true attitudes and beliefs about the principles will be revealed in later group sessions.

6. *Respect the men's disagreements and differing views.* Avoid power struggles. Do not pressure the men to agree with these principles at this time. Simply allow them to state how they feel about the principles, and ask them what thoughts or experiences shape their feelings. Your main job during this activity is to state the program philosophy and what opinions they can expect from you, not to have them parrot responses they think you expect of them.

7. *Deal with some of the resistance to these principles during individual counseling sessions.* While an individual counseling session is not a forum to convince a client to believe the program's principles, it is an opportunity to observe his reactions to them. Explaining the principles in the individual sessions may take the edge off some of the resistance. Again, you are reinforcing your views and what the men can expect from you in the group setting.

8. *The eight program principles will surface often throughout the group sessions.* During all of the activities in subsequent group sessions, at least one of these eight principles can be referenced. Use them as often as possible, always stating that these are your views. It helps to rephrase them occasionally, to keep the information fresh.

Notes, comments, and observations:

Participant's Workbook Sample

Goals

In this activity, you will:

1. Learn and understand the program's philosophical basis.

2. Discuss whether you agree with the eight program principles.

3. Talk more with other men in the group.

4. Begin to develop your own philosophy of violence and abuse.

WORKSHEET 2   Eight Program Principles

1. **Violence has rewards and consequences.**
   What are some rewards?
   What are some consequences?

2. **Violence can be passed on from generation to generation.**
   How?

3. **Violence is reinforced by our society.**
   In what ways?

4. **Violence can be unlearned. There are other ways to express feelings. There are alternatives to controlling people and situations.**
   What are some alternatives?

5. **I am responsible for my behavior.**
   In what ways?

6. **Provocation does not justify violence.**
   When is violence justified?

7. **100 percent rule: I am 100 percent responsible for my side of a relationship.**
   When are you *not* responsible for your behavior in the relationship?

8. **The only person I can control is myself.**
   Who else can I control? When?

May Not Be Reproduced

WORSHEET 3   My Philosophy of Abuse and Violence

Describe your philosophy of abuse and violence below.

1. Abuse means:

2. Violence means:

3. People are abusive because:

4. How does society view abuse and violence? How can you tell?

5. How do the media (newspapers, television, radio, commercials, magazines, advertisements) show violence and abuse?

6. Why do people continue to be abusive?

7. When, if at all, is it okay for you to be abusive or violent?

8. What are your rewards for abuse and violence in the above situations?

9. What are possible negative consequences in these situations?

10. In what specific situations is it okay for you to hurt someone? When does a person deserve to be abused?

11. How much is a person responsible for his or her own behavior? Explain your answer.

12. If person A abuses person B, who is to blame for the abuse?

13. What, if any, are the reasons to blame the abused person or both people for the abuse?

14. How much can one person control another person?

May Not Be Reproduced

Men's Rules
about Men

Goals

In this activity, participants will:

1. Identify social, familial, educational, peer, and media messages about how men should or should not act.

2. Understand how these messages influence their behaviors.

3. Identify the advantages and disadvantages of maintaining (believing in and living out) these messages.

4. Identify their beliefs about who men are and how men should act.

5. Identify society's expectations and their personal beliefs about how women should or should not act.

6. Understand how these beliefs affect their behaviors toward women.

7. Increase their awareness of sexist attitudes and beliefs and how these values affect men's behaviors toward women.

8. List and increase alternative, positive messages about being a man.

Required Worksheets

Men's Rules about Men (Worksheet 4)
Men's Rules about Women (Worksheet 5)
Summary of Men's Rules (Worksheet 6)

Format

Begin by asking the men to turn to the worksheet, Men's Rules about Men. Ask the men to answer the first two questions as completely as possible. Let them know that in ten minutes you will ask them to share their ideas with each other.

Have the men form pairs and read their lists to each other. Allow no more than five minutes to do this.

Write "Men's Rules about Men" on the chalkboard. Ask each man to read aloud from his answers to questions one and two. Select a volunteer to write those answers on the chalkboard, and ask another volunteer to record the lists on paper for distribution later.

After all the men have read from their lists, ask the following questions:

- Are there any themes in what you see on the board?

- What is surprising?

- What is not surprising?

- How would you summarize this list in two or three words?

- How does it feel to see this list?

Next, give the men ten minutes to answer worksheet questions three and four. Have them pair up and share their answers for five minutes. On another part of the chalkboard, write "What I Gain" and "What I Lose." As before, have the men read their responses aloud and use volunteers to record the responses on the chalkboard and paper. After all the men have spoken, repeat the above questions ("Are there any themes? What is surprising," and so forth).

Now that you have listed Men's Rules and their associated advantages and disadvantages, help the men explore the consequences of changing the rules. Write on the chalkboard,

If I break the above rules:

What do I gain (benefits)?	What do I lose (consequences)?

Ask the men to suggest gains and losses for breaking the rules they listed in "Men's Rules about Men." Record their responses as in the previous two exercises, and encourage the men to write these responses on their worksheets as well (questions five and six). After the men have completed their suggestions, lead a discussion by asking the same questions used previously ("Are there any themes? What is surprising," and so forth).

Finally, have the men brainstorm alternative rules and beliefs about masculinity. Ask them to write these alternative rules in their workbooks, focusing on suggestions that nurture positive attitudes. Also ask the men how these messages affect their behaviors. For example, with the new messages, how often would they cry? Show other emotions? To whom would they show emotions? How would these new messages change the way they demonstrate to others their beliefs about being men?

Ask the men to turn to the Men's Rules about Women worksheet. Give the men ten minutes to answer the questions. Explain that they will share their answers in the group.

At the top of the chalkboard, write "Men's Rules about Women" and "Society's Rules about Women." As the men share their answers, write their rules on the board, and have a volunteer record these on a sheet of paper.

Ask the following questions:

- How similar are the men's rules for women and society's rules for women?

- What are the overriding themes of the rules for women when set down by men? When set down by society?

- How does it feel to see these lists?

- How do these lists and the lists about men compare?

Next, have the men turn to the worksheet, Summary of Men's Rules. Ask the men to answer these questions at home. Explain that they will share their responses in the next session. (At the next session, be sure to distribute copies of all the lists and review them. Ask if there are any additions.)

Close the session by asking some of the questions on the worksheet, Summary of Men's Rules. Discuss how social and personal attitudes affect men's behavior. Examine the ways this exercise reveals that our attitudes about men and women set up a system of power, control, and oppression.

Summarize your observations of *how* these men talked about Men's Rules. Were they able to discuss them openly? Did they joke around or make inappropriate comments? Reveal some of your concerns and opinions. State that many of these issues will be coming up on various levels in the forthcoming sessions.

Issues

1. *We recommend using this activity within the first few meetings.* It helps set the tone for future group sessions, yet it is not too threatening for men to talk about, if given careful preparation and delivery.

2. *Some men may resist offering any ideas or opinions.* They may feel ashamed of their views or fear that others will laugh at them. Respectfully encourage interaction among the group members. Have the men ask each other questions. Some men may still be too angry to express their beliefs. Encourage them to think about their negative perspective and how long they want to stay angry.

3. *Some men will state that they already reject society's messages about men and women.* Acknowledge their ability to maintain a value which contradicts much of what other men believe or society reinforces. Remind them that they are brainstorming general messages and will examine personal beliefs soon. Briefly discuss how men have become violent, referring to the principle that violence is learned. Explain that some men may reject society's message but still be violent toward a partner.

4. *The questions in this exercise progress in difficulty.* You may need to rephrase some questions to make sure everyone understands. Discuss the rewards and consequences of violent behavior. Examine how personal heroes, movie heroes, sports figures, or adults they saw while growing up were given rewards or consequences for their violent behavior.

5. *When discussing their childhood experiences, be sensitive to your clients' family of origin issues.* Sometimes you can draw men into the discussion by using a statement such as "Some men who came from violent homes made themselves a promise that they would never be abusive themselves." Use the individual counseling sessions to determine what information you can draw upon in the group. Respect your clients' privacy; always ask the men to share personal information only if they are willing. There will be times later on when the men will be asked to be more open (for example, when describing their most hurtful incident). If men bring up personal histories of childhood violence during group, relate those experiences to your point. Refer to the principle that violence can be passed from generation to generation.

6. *Some men may see some connections between the Men's Rules and violent behavior during this session, only to lose this insight in later group sessions.* Be patient with the men, yourself, and the process. If you feel frustrated or impatient because your clients do not seem to change their views, seek support from your colleagues.

7. *Some men will resent and resist any positive discussion of this topic.* Let these group members vent some of their feelings. If possible, apply some of their comments toward the activities. Some men will ask, "Why talk about men when the problem is women?" Help the group identify the rule or attitude at the source of such thinking: Women are the cause of men's abusive behavior. Reaffirm that the only person a man can control is himself, and this includes his reactions to what women do.

Notes, comments, and observations:

Participant's Workbook Sample

Goals

In this activity, you will:

1. Identify some messages about how men should or should not act.

2. Understand how these messages influence your behaviors.

3. Identify the advantages and disadvantages of believing in and acting on these messages.

4. Identify your beliefs about who men are and how men should act.

5. Identify society's expectations and your personal beliefs about how women should or should not act.

6. Understand how these beliefs affect your behaviors toward women.

7. Increase your awareness of sexist attitudes and how they affect men's behaviors toward women.

8. List and increase alternative, positive messages about being a man.

WORKSHEET 4   Men's Rules about Men

1. List society's rules, traditions, and messages that define how a man should act, think, or be. Also list examples of how a man should *not* act, think, or be. How are men shown in the media (commercials, movies, cartoons)? Who are boys' heroes? Examples of such rules include: *Men should not cry. Men should not show their emotions. Men need to be in control.*

2. List the messages your family gave you about being a man. List the messages about how a man should act. Who were your heroes when growing up? How did these heroes get the job done?

3. List your rewards for maintaining and living by these rules. What do you gain from these rules?

4. List the consequences of following these rules. What do you lose or miss out on?

5. Do you find more rewards or negative consequences for the rules? If there are more rewards, why change your attitude? List some rewards you may receive if you challenge these rules.

6. List some negative consequences of breaking Men's Rules about Men.

7. What are some better rules and attitudes for men? How can you encourage these attitudes in yourself? Where will you get support for believing and acting on these new attitudes?

8. How can you encourage more positive attitudes about men among other men? Among boys, such as sons and nephews?

May Not Be Reproduced

WORKSHEET 5   Men's Rules about Women

1. What are men's expectations and rules about how women should act and think? Examples of such rules include: *Women need to be protected. Women are the weaker sex.*

2. List your beliefs about women: How they should act, think, and be. How similar is this list to the list of men's expectations of women?

3. How can you encourage more positive attitudes among men toward women? What might you say to a male friend of yours who makes a sexist comment or who puts down a woman? Would your reactions change if the woman he was putting down was your mother? Your sister? Your daughter?

WORKSHEET 6   Summary of Men's Rules

Compare all of your lists of attitudes toward women and men.

1. What are the similarities?

2. What are the differences?

3. Which expectations are realistic?

4. Which expectations are unrealistic?

5. How are your attitudes about women and men affected by society?

6. How do you view women? Negatively? Positively?

7. How do you demonstrate these attitudes? (For example, do you tell jokes that put women down? Do you believe women are bad and out to get men? Do you tell a male friend that you are offended by his remarks that put women down? Would you call 911 if you hear or see a man abusing a woman?)

8. How do you want your daughter to relate to men when she is an adult?

9. What are your attitudes toward your mother, wife, girlfriend, women coworkers, women you meet casually?

10. What are the differences in how you view these women? What are the similarities?

May Not Be Reproduced

House of Abuse

Goals

In this activity, participants will:

1. Extend the definition of abuse beyond the four categories of verbal, physical, emotional, and sexual.

2. Identify the purpose of abusive behaviors.

3. Increase their personal awareness of abusive behaviors.

4. Understand that changing abusive behavior is an ongoing process.

5. Understand that abuse is abuse no matter what form it takes.

Required Worksheet

House of Abuse (Worksheet 7)

Format

On the chalkboard, draw a large house with nine rooms. (See the worksheet, House of Abuse, for an example.) Ask what four types of abuse we most commonly think of. Label four rooms "verbal," "physical," "emotional," and "sexual" abuse. Ask the men to turn to the worksheet, House of Abuse. Tell them to complete the worksheet as they discuss types of abuse.

Ask the men for examples of verbal abuse. Record both specific suggestions and general ones. In other words, write "put-downs" and "name-calling," as well as "lazy" and "stupid."

Follow the same process for the rooms labeled "physical," "emotional" (also known as psychological or mental) and "sexual" abuse.

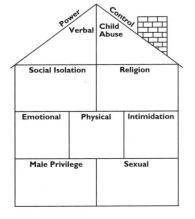

House of Abuse

After all four of these rooms have been filled, suggest that there are other categories of abuse. These categories of abuse include isolation, intimidation, religious, child, male privilege, and economic. Label each of the remaining rooms with one of these or a similar descriptor. Fill in the rooms, one category at a time, with specific and general examples. Offer suggestions of abusive situations and ask in what room(s) they may fit. Ask if other rooms should be added, and add them to the house as needed.

Next, have the group members discuss how they feel about what they see on the chalkboard. In what ways do some of the rooms connect, overlap, or share examples? Have the group investigate the possibility of what happens if they concentrate on "cleaning" only one room (for example, physical abuse) without cleaning the whole house (that is, halting the specific abuse without changing an abusive approach to relationships).

What will eventually happen? Point out that if one type of violence is accepted and justified, it's probably only a matter of time before other types of violence occur. Ask the group which form of abuse is worse. After they answer, point out that abuse is abuse no matter what form it takes. All types of abuse destroy relationships.

Ask the group to discuss the purpose of abuse. Explain that power and control rest on the roof of the house, propped up by all the abuse within. Ask what one potentially gains by being abusive. Help them recognize that they gain power and control through abuse. Encourage them to think about what they also might gain that they *don't* want.

Next, ask what is in the basement of the house. Lead the men to talk about how feelings are in the basement. Explain that they can strengthen the foundation of the house by expressing their feelings in a nonabusive manner. When men ignore, deny, minimize, or refuse to deal with their feelings, they limit their choices for responding to situations. As a result, they act out using violent behaviors. This is a good time to revisit the program principles, "I am responsible for myself" and "The only person I can control is myself."

Discuss at length the interconnectedness of the rooms. Help the men develop insights into how abuse in one area will eventually affect other areas. Explain that the long-term goal of this program is to clean one's house completely. Explore their ideas on the following:

- How long would cleaning the house take?

- What do you replace the abusive behaviors with?

- Who is responsible for cleaning the house?

- Who can control the cleaning?

- What are some alternatives to abuse that help us deal with our feelings more effectively and efficiently?

- What is it like being a child in this house?

Emphasize that this is a lifelong issue for all men, and that they need to work on all rooms at the same time. Some men tend to say that once they have stopped being physically abusive, they are done. But the House of Abuse gives group members a broader picture of abuse: Whether verbal, physical, or through the exercise of male privilege, abuse is abuse. Explain that once a man has built his house with abusive behaviors, he can justify moving the use of abuse from one room to the next. The *only* solution is for him to work at keeping all the rooms clean.

Finally, help the men understand that they cannot fairly determine whether their actions have been abusive. The decision that an action is abusive rests with the person who is at the receiving end of the behavior. To stop abusing, the group members will need to listen to other people's observations, feelings, and reactions to their behavior.

Issues

1. *Some clients may try to shock you with their abusive language or "war stories."* Limit how graphic they may be when writing or talking about their answers to questions. Some clients use offensive language to get a reaction from you or the group. State clearly when they have crossed the line into being abusive of others by using inappropriate or disrespectful language.

2. *Be open to all specific and general examples.* Allow the clients time to build their own definition of abuse. Help them clarify their definitions of abuse by asking questions. For example, if someone suggests "silent treatment," ask how this behavior is abusive.

3. *This is a powerful exercise.* Most clients have not viewed abuse in such broad terms. They may feel overwhelmed and shamed by what they see on the board. Give them time to discuss these feelings and how they will deal with them in the short-term (when they leave the session) and in the long-term. Help them understand how this broadened definition of abuse can improve their life and the lives of their loved ones. (Note: Some men may become angered or depressed by this exercise; question those who seem to be at risk of endangering themselves or others.)

4. *Clients may have difficulty giving examples for some of the rooms.* Be patient and remember that this may be the first time they have seen abuse discussed so broadly. They may not know how to respond or be confused by your terms. Use your own examples or ask the group to define or rephrase the types of abuse. Keep asking for their views until you're sure they understand. Some of the men may still be in denial of their abusive behavior. It may take some time for them to accept this information.

5. *The "male privilege" category is often the most difficult to fully explain.* Help the men understand by bringing up terms like "boss" and "king of the castle." More subtle examples of male privilege, such as higher wages, easier access to jobs, and so forth, will challenge you and the group. Allow them to express their views on the subtleties of this category. Avoid power struggles, but provide many examples and clearly state your views.

6. *Focus your discussion on power and control as primary motivators for using abusive actions.* Have the clients explain and discuss how power and control are related to abuse. Talk about the rewards and conse-

quences of being abusive. Challenge any abusive attitudes with your observations and experience. Avoid accusations, preaching, and power struggles.

7. *One or two group members may maintain that they have never committed an abusive act listed in the House of Abuse.* Ask these particular clients to clarify their views. Be aware of the shame and anger they may feel about the subject and what is written on the board. Use the group process as much as possible; ask the group their reactions to these claims. Ultimately, you may need to offer your observations and move on. A client's denial of his behavior can be frustrating, so be patient with yourself. Get support from colleagues and supervisors to deal with your frustrations and to reevaluate your expectations of resistant group members.

8. *Some men may want you to move into talking about what they should do when they feel like being abusive.* Timing is important; if you move beyond this activity too fast—without adequately addressing a definition of violence—you may become sidetracked, and eventually you will have to come back to define abuse clearly.

9. *Use the phrase, "We are looking at what could be abusive to someone."* Emphasize that one behavior could have different impacts depending on both the intent and the individual. For example, tickling can sometimes be playful behavior, but it could also be abusive. Ask the men, "When could tickling be used in an abusive way?" Also explain that the men need to be aware of how others experience their behavior. For example, if a man decides to cope with his anger by cleaning his guns, his partner is probably going to see his actions as threatening even if he does not mean them to be. Thus, he must be aware of the impact of his behavior *regardless* of his intent. This issue can best be discussed while filling in the room of emotional abuse.

Notes, comments, and observations:

Participant's Workbook Sample

Goals

In this activity, you will:

1. Extend the definition of abuse beyond the four categories of verbal, physical, emotional, and sexual.

2. Identify the purpose of abusive behaviors.

3. Increase your personal awareness of abusive behaviors.

4. Understand that changing abusive behavior is an ongoing process.

5. Understand that abuse is abuse no matter what form it takes.

WORKSHEET 7 House of Abuse

1. List examples of the types of abuse in each room.

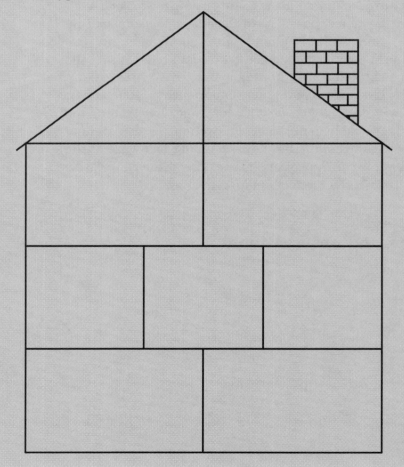

(continued)

2. How are the rooms similar? How are they connected?

3. What would happen if you totally cleaned out three or four rooms but left the other rooms full?

4. How does abuse support power and control?

5. What is in the basement of your house? What are the feelings?

6. Are there other rooms you could add to the house?

7. What feelings do you have when you see this house full of abuse?

8. What have you learned from looking at abuse this way?

9. What do you need to do to clean your house and how can you take care of yourself in this process?

May Not Be Reproduced

The Pattern of Abuse

Goals

In this activity, participants will:

1. Better understand the dynamics of abuse and how abuse reoccurs.

2. Understand the three stages of the abuse cycle and how these stages are demonstrated.

3. Understand at what points new decisions need to be made so no abuse occurs.

Required Worksheet

Pattern of Abuse (Worksheet 8)

Format

Introduce the three stages of the pattern of abuse: escalation, blowout, and after behaviors. Have the group give examples of each stage. Discuss how these stages eventually occur again and again unless something interrupts the process.

Ask the men to turn to the Pattern of Abuse worksheet. Hand out some crayons, markers, pens, or pencils. Explain that they will have fifteen minutes to draw their own pattern of abuse. Have them illustrate their escalation, blowout, and after behaviors, as well as how the pattern begins again. Let them know they can draw or write whatever they want about the cycle of abuse, as long as it makes sense to them. Let them use symbols, stick figures, designs, words, or numbers in their picture. Explain that they will share their picture with the rest of the group.

After they have finished their drawings, ask for a volunteer to talk about his picture. Let him know that the purpose of the discussion is for him to understand his own pattern of abuse. Here are some questions you can ask to elicit his explanation:

- Where is the escalation phase? Blowout phase? After behaviors phase?

- How do the after behaviors tie back into the escalation?

- What does the picture show? Who is in it?

- What is in the picture? How are colors, shading, or strength of line used to depict elements of the pattern of abuse?

Encourage the group to ask questions about the picture, too. Repeat this process until everyone has shared his picture. Ask if there are any themes, common threads, or similarities in the pictures.

When everyone has shared, explain that men often describe their violent behavior this way: "Everything is going well. All of a sudden I get upset at my partner and I lose it. Then everything is fine again." Draw Figure A on the chalk board.

Figure A

Point out that when some men begin to look at their violent behaviors more closely, they are able to identify a specific pattern of behaviors. Draw Figure B on the chalkboard.

Write in the three stages of the pattern. Point out some of the similarities between this pattern and the pictures the group members drew.

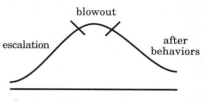

Figure B

Explain that over time, if the abusive person receives no help, the cycle will look like Figure C. The abuse becomes more frequent and more serious over time.

Describe how abuse can and often does occur in each stage of the cycle, even though it looks as if the abuse only occurs in the blowout stage. Explain how after behaviors are often manipulative ways of being forgiven or "felt sorry for." Explain that these manipulations are a form of abuse, too, because they shift the focus from the victim of the abuse to the perpetrator, which is yet another form of maintaining control through blame.

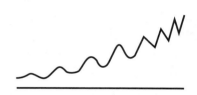

Figure C

During the escalation stage, name-calling, grabbing, put-downs, threats, and so forth are the most common forms of abuse. Let the men know that their mission is to take care of their feelings and express them appropriately *before* the men use these or any other abusive behaviors. Tell them they'll learn specific techniques for this in future sessions.

Ask the men for examples of situations that add to the frustration and escalation phase. Emphasize that this phase can be quick or gradual; it could take a few minutes to several months. Explain that the blowout phase is when the most violence occurs, and it does not have to be physical abuse; it can be verbal, emotional, or sexual abuse. Sexual abuse may occur prior to the blowout as the partner believes being sexual with the man may prevent the blowout phase. The man often uses this as an opportunity for rough sex. Sexual abuse often occurs after the blowout, when the man feels bad about his behavior and believes being sexual will make up for it.

The after behaviors are those ways the man attempts to make up, trying to get his partner to "forgive and forget." Emphasize that the men need to be mindful of their feelings during this time. The man's outward appearance may be calm and collected, but his partner feels no real safety to be angry. The man needs to identify and monitor his anger as he may not totally de-escalate during this part of the pattern. Ask the men what they have done or ways they have felt during the after behavior phase.

Conclude this activity by summarizing the pattern of abuse, its various phases, and your hope that they can do something different early in the process of escalation to take care of themselves. Emphasize that they need to focus on the escalation phase. It is critical that they become aware of their early signs of escalation; if they are successful in this, they will reduce the risk of reaching the blowout phase or the after behaviors.

Issues

1. *The group members may be hesitant and resist drawing.* Reassure them that they will not be graded on these drawings. Give them permission to make their drawing as simple or complex as they desire.

2. *Some men resist the concept of escalation. They defend their abuse by saying that they just "blow up," "lose it," or "act on reflex."* Have the group identify the situations when they feel they just "react." Help them understand that there is an escalation stage which leads to the blowout. Help them identify some of their personal signals in the escalation phase.

3. *Some men simply refuse to do this activity.* Respectfully, have the group review the expectations of participation or other program policies discussed in the activity, Introduction to Group. Clarify the reasons for this exercise on the pattern of abuse. Ask if they understand or what their concerns are about this activity. (For more help, refer to **Working with Resistant Clients**, page 17.)

4. *Group members may want to focus on their partners' behaviors rather than their own patterns.* Explore how the men felt as they experienced the stages. Explain that these feelings are their feelings and this is their pattern, not their partners'. The feelings are signals that they must take care of themselves without being abusive. Revisit the principle about who they can and cannot control.

5. *Some men may believe that this is "just the way things are."* Challenge their perspective by asking questions such as: Do you like what you are doing? Do you believe you can change? Do things have to stay the same? Point out that this sense of hopelessness is an obstacle to change. It is a choice to keep things the same or to rationalize one's own violent behaviors.

6. *Clients may feel shame, anger, frustration, powerlessness, grief, and so forth when looking at their pattern of abuse.* Explore these feelings, because denying them may impede some men's acceptance of the stages of abuse. Help each man get support from the group for admitting these feelings and talking about what can be done with them.

7. *Men usually seem to benefit from visualizing the pattern of abuse.* The identification of the stages helps clients see ways out of the pattern. Thus, they are closer to choosing options other than abuse. It is more important that the men see that a pattern exists than that they all agree on the exact shape of the pattern.

8. *Emphasize that the men must learn to identify their escalation signals.* Explain that this pattern will help them understand themselves better. Attention to the signals can prevent them from feeling trapped, hopeless, and powerless. The earlier they identify their signals within the pattern, the sooner they can begin to take care of themselves. A man who is acting abusively is *not* taking care of himself. The longer he stays in a situation believing "it's not so bad yet," the closer he is to trouble. He will have more choices (or feel that he does) if he identifies his signals earlier.

◆◆◆

Notes, comments, and observations:

Goals

In this activity, you will:

1. Better understand how abuse happens again and again.

2. Learn the three stages of the abuse cycle and what these stages look like.

3. Understand at what points you need to make new decisions so no abuse occurs.

WORSHEET 8   Pattern of Abuse

Draw your own pattern of abusive behavior. Show the escalation, blowout, after behaviors, and how the pattern begins again. Use stick figures, symbols, numbers, words, designs, or whatever makes sense to you.

Goals

In this activity, participants will:

1. Identify and understand what they think and feel and how their body reacts when they begin to get angry or upset.

2. Identify words, phrases, sentences, situations, subject matter, or times of the day in which they feel confused, tense, angry, or upset.

3. Increase their willingness to accept what other people tell them about their behavior.

Escalation Signals (Worksheet 9)
Feelings Words (Worksheet 10)
Signals Monitoring Log (Worksheet 11)

**Required
Worksheets**

◆◆◆

Ask the men to turn to the Escalation Signals worksheet. Give them ten minutes to fill it out. Explain that you will ask them to share what they have written. As the men fill out their worksheets write the following across the top of the chalkboard:

Format

Physical signals	Thought signals	Emotional signals	Red flag words & phrases	Red flag situations

Ask the group to share some of what they have written in these categories, and write their responses on the board. Ask if some of these ideas suggest ways that they can identify when they are feeling tense, upset, confused, or whatever other feelings lead to escalation. For help, suggest the men look at the Feelings Words worksheet.

Explain how all of these signals are indicators that they may be escalating into the blowout stage of the cycle of abuse. Let them know they have choices once they identify these signals and understand what they mean. Remind them that only they can monitor and control their behaviors, thoughts, and feelings. Relate this to the principles of controlling oneself and personal responsibility. Remind them that these are their signals, not those of their partners.

Explore some of the obstacles to identifying these signals in an escalating situation. These may include:

- Power struggles

- Emotional investment in "winning" an argument

- Feeling ashamed about past behaviors

At the end of this exercise, have the men turn to the Signals Monitoring Log. Ask them to answer the first two questions of this worksheet during this session. Tell the men to be as specific as possible. Then ask them to choose a feeling (from the vocabulary sheet or on their own) to monitor for the next two weeks. Explain that they will share the information from this worksheet with the rest of the group at a later session.

Have each man decide on a safe person to talk to about this exercise. Explain that they will need to ask this person to observe their behavior and give them feedback, particularly about how he or she may fear the particular behavior. Suggest that they show the person the worksheet to help him or her understand the process.

Follow-Up

During the follow-up session to this exercise, have the men discuss the feelings they were monitoring for the past two weeks. Then have them read their responses. Ask some of the following questions:

- How often did you have this feeling?

- Did your body have similar reactions each time?

- Did you have similar self-talk each time?

- What other feelings did you have?

- How similar were the red flag words or situations?

- What have you learned from this monitoring?

- What other feelings would be helpful to monitor?

- How difficult was it to accept other people's observations about your behavior without explaining or defending your position?

Ask how it felt to do this exercise and what they learned from it. Examine areas that were new for them. Summarize why it is important for the men to identify and understand their signals: When they learn their signals, they can take more responsibility for their choice of abusive or nonabusive behavior. In addition, listening to other people's observations about their behaviors does not have to be shaming or hurtful, but can be a helpful growing process.

◆◆◆

Issues

1. *Initially, many men state that their body does not respond to anger.* Accept this as a possibility. Often men have not examined how their body reacts to tension or anger. One or two men will usually be able to identify some way their body reacts. Encourage others to expand on this list: sweaty palms, dry mouth, fast heartbeat, and so forth.

2. *Clients also have difficulty identifying the thoughts they typically have while angry.* Again, capitalize on any responses and offer suggestions to help the group come up with more ideas.

3. *Allow the men to choose as many feelings from the Feelings Words worksheet as possible.* This may seem time consuming, but it gives the men the opportunity to talk about feelings. Often they have difficulty identifying much more than "angry" or "frustrated." This worksheet offers them more alternatives. It can be used for other activities as well.

4. *Have the men focus on red flag words, sentences, and situations that really "pushed their buttons."* This helps them continue to focus on themselves. Explain that *they* are in control of these buttons and whether the buttons can be pushed. Review the principles of control and personal responsibility.

5. *We strongly recommend that you require your clients to complete the Signals Monitoring Log as part of your program.* This activity helps the men gain some insight into and objectivity about their emotions, often for the first time in their life. Be clear about what you expect them to record during the two weeks of monitoring, and what they will have to present during the follow-up session. Give alternatives for those who cannot read and write, such as use of an audiocassette or a daily phone-in to a counselor, volunteer, or peer from the group.

6. *The men will have a difficult time asking others to observe their behaviors, as required in the Signals Monitoring Log.* Explain that in order for them to change their pattern of abuse, they will need to learn to listen to other people's observations about their behavior. They may resist this exercise because it makes them feel vulnerable. Talk about how it will feel to have someone observe them. Discuss some of the obstacles to listening to another person's observations: the observations might be painfully true; they might not like what they hear; they might not believe the person. Talk about how they might react after

hearing the observations: they might get angry, yell, ask questions defensively, or deny that the observations are true. If a man states there is no one to give observations, have him partner with another group member.

◆◆◆

Notes, comments, and observations:

Participant's Workbook Sample

Goals

In this activity, you will:

1. Identify what you think and feel and how your body reacts when you begin to get angry or upset.

2. Identify words, phrases, sentences, subject matter, situations, or times of the day when you feel confused, tense, angry, or upset.

3. Increase your willingness to accept what other people tell you about your behavior.

WORKSHEET 9	Escalation Signals

Make a list of the signals (or cues) that you are getting upset.

1. *Physical Signals.* When you get angry, how does your body react? What is your body telling you? What are you doing?

2. *Thought Signals.* What suspicions, assumptions, thoughts, and self-talk get you upset?

3. *Emotional Signals.* What feelings do you have before and during the times when you are upset? What feelings do you have before and during the times when you are verbally, physically, or sexually abusive? Use the Feelings Words worksheet to help you identify your feelings.

4. *Red Flag Words and Sentences.* What words, phrases, and sentences get you upset?

5. *Red Flag Situations.* What are the "hot" situations, topics, places, and times of day?

May Not Be Reproduced

WORKSHEET 10 Feelings Words

Emotional signals are the feelings you have before, during, or after the times that you are abusive. There are names for these signals. "Angry" or "upset" are the easy ones. Try to identify the most exact name for the feeling you are having by looking at the list of feelings under the category for that feeling.

Happy	Sad		Angry		Scared	Confused
Excited	Devastated	Disheartened	Strangled	Resentful	Fearful	Bewildered
Elated	Hopeless	Despised	Furious	Disgusted	Panicky	Trapped
Exuberant	Sorrowful	Disappointed	Seething	Smothered	Afraid	Immobilized
Ecstatic	Depressed	Upset	Enraged	Frustrated	Shocked	Directionless
Terrific	Wounded	Inadequate	Hostile	Stifled	Overwhelmed	Stagnant
Jubilant	Hurt	Dismal	Vengeful	Offended	Intimidated	Flustered
Enthusiastic	Drained	Unappreciated	Incensed	Controlled	Desperate	Baffled
Loved	Defeated	Discouraged	Abused	Peeved	Frantic	Constricted
Thrilled	Exhausted	Ashamed	Hateful	Annoyed	Terrified	Troubled
Uplifted	Helpless	Distressed	Humiliated	Agitated	Vulnerable	Ambivalent
Marvelous	Crushed	Distant	Sabotaged	Irritated	Horrified	Awkward
Justified	Worthless	Disillusioned	Betrayed	Exasperated	Petrified	Puzzled
Resolved	Uncared-for	Lonely	Repulsed	Harassed	Appalled	Disorganized
Valued	Dejected	Neglected	Rebellious	Anguished	Full of dread	Foggy
Gratified	Rejected	Resigned	Pissed off	Deceived	Tormented	Perplexed
Encouraged	Humbled	Islanded	Outraged	Aggravated	Tense	Hesitant
Optimistic	Empty	Regretful	Fuming	Perturbed	Threatened	Torn
Joyful	Miserable	Alienated	Exploited	Provoked	Uneasy	Misunderstood
Proud	Distraught	Isolated	Throttled	Dominated	Defensive	Doubtful
Cheerful	Deserted	Drained	Mad	Coerced	Insecure	Bothered
Relieved	Grievous	Slighted	Spiteful	Cheated	Skeptical	Undecided
Assured	Burdened	Degraded	Patronized	Uptight	Apprehensive	Uncomfortable
Determined	Demoralized	Deprived	Vindictive	Dismayed	Suspicious	Uncertain
Grateful	Condemned	Disturbed	Used	Tolerant	Alarmed	Surprised
Appreciated	Terrible	Abandoned	Repulsed	Displeased	Shaken	Unsettled
Confident	Unwanted	Sorry	Ridiculed		Swamped	Unsure
Respected	Unloved	Lost			Startled	Distracted
Admired	Mournful	Bad			Guarded	
Accepted	Pitiful	Disenchanted			Stunned	
Amused	Discarded	Deflated			Awed	
Delighted	Disgraced	Apathetic			Reluctant	
Alive					Anxious	
Fulfilled					Impatient	
Tranquil					Shy	
Content					Nervous	
Relaxed					Unsure	
Glad					Timid	
Good					Concerned	
Satisfied					Perplexed	
Peaceful					Doubtful	
Hopeful						
Fortunate						
Pleased						
Flattered						

WORKSHEET II   Signals Monitoring Log

1. Who can you ask to observe your behavior and tell you what they see?

2. Name one or more feelings you want to monitor to help you learn about your escalation signals:

3. During the next two weeks, log your signals in the chart below every time you experience the feeling you want to monitor. Make a new chart if you run out of space.

Date	What you are thinking	How your body is reacting	Your feelings	Your red flag words and phrases	Your red flag situations and subjects

May Not Be Reproduced

Responsibility Plan

Goals

In this activity, participants will:

1. Increase the use of nonabusive options when dealing with feelings that have led to the desire to control their partners.

2. Develop a responsibility plan with several options to interrupt the escalation stage.

3. Develop a respectful way to communicate with a partner or ex-partner after using the responsibility plan.

4. Understand the obstacles to leaving an argument and develop some techniques to overcome those obstacles.

Required Worksheets

Responsibility Plan (Worksheet 12)
Responsibility Plan Monitoring Worksheet (Worksheet 13)

Format

Discuss the need for blueprints when building a house or manuals when fixing a car. These plans identify areas to troubleshoot when something needs changing or fixing. Explain that just as a manual can help us fix a house or car, a plan can help us rebuild a house of abuse. This is the purpose of the responsibility plan. It is a tool to reduce the risk of using abusive behaviors.

Emphasize that a responsibility plan does not solve arguments or problems, but it does help break the pattern of abuse so that progress can be made on solving relationship problems at a less volatile time.

Ask the men to turn to the Responsibility Plan worksheet, and lead the group through a discussion that answers the questions on the worksheet. First, have the group brainstorm actions they have taken in the past to deal with their feelings in a nonabusive manner. Write these ideas on the chalkboard and encourage the men to write the ideas that fit for them on their worksheets. Explain that they will be required to talk about their personal responsibility plan at a follow-up session.

Next, introduce the idea that a *time-out*—physically leaving a potentially abusive situation—can stop a man from escalating to abuse. Discuss and list some of the obstacles that keep the men from taking a time-out. These may include challenges from his partner as well as his own self-talk or beliefs. Some examples are:

- "This is my house!"
- "I make the money, she should go!"
- "You're not going to do this to me!"
- "She's not going to call the police on me!"
- "I'll show you!"
- Revenge.
- Lack of money.
- Fear of losing the relationship or getting divorced.
- Fear of what others (family, friends) will think.
- Need to prove masculinity.
- The partner accuses the man of cheating on her during a time-out.
- The partner threatens, "If you leave, don't come back!"

Point out that these messages are often false and prevent a man from leaving a potentially abusive situation. Explain that they need new messages to replace the old ones, messages that don't lead to a sense of being trapped. Discuss and list alternative messages. Some examples include:

- "I need to take care of myself."
- "I don't want to end up in jail."
- "I don't deserve to be hurt like this."
- "When I leave I am taking care of myself and my family."
- "I need to leave so I don't hurt the people I love."

To help make the case for taking a time-out, review the negative consequences of staying in a potentially abusive situation. Then give an overview of the actual time-out plan and what it entails:

- How to know when to take a time-out (signals).
- How to take a time-out without being abusive.
- What to do during a time-out.
- How to reconnect after the time-out; and if there is to be any contact with the partner again, how to attempt to reconnect with her directly.

Explain that for a man who has been abusive, time-outs are nonnegotiable. This is best for both the man and his partner. Because partners may see a time-out as "running away," each man should discuss his time-out plan with his partner when both of them are calm—not when either one is upset or when they're involved in an argument. He needs to explain what a time-out is, as well as what he will do and where he will go during a time-out. Finally, the couple has to negotiate ways the man can know it is safe to return.

Remind the men of the escalation signals they became aware of during the activity, Escalation Signals. These are the signals that tell them they need a time-out. Invite a volunteer to read from his list of signals. Then continue until everyone has read.

Next, discuss their plans for leaving. Explore options for leaving in positive ways. Have them commit to at least three possibilities. Then have them identify the specific self-talk they will use next time they find themselves in a potentially abusive situation, drawing from the list they created earlier in the session. Discuss at length where they will go and what they will do when they take a time-out. Ask them to be specific.

Finally, emphasize the importance of talking to or being with someone during a time-out. Explain that they should choose someone who can listen without giving them permission to be abusive or telling them it's okay if they have been abusive. Explain that because the need for a time-out arises when they are upset, they need to be prepared with a list of people who they can contact quickly, either by phone or dropping in.

The next step in the responsibility plan is to reestablish contact with the partner after a time-out. The men need to identify the internal signals that tell them they can communicate with their partner without being abusive. Help them identify what those signals might be: better self-talk, feeling more relaxed, feeling less trapped, and so forth. If their signals are still in an escalated state, it is not safe for them to return.

Brainstorm and list ways the men can reconnect safely and respectfully with their partner. Some suggestions: discuss the plan prior to taking any time-outs so she knows where he'll be; call from wherever he is to see if he can return; ask someone else to call and check with her; have a prearranged signal for when it is okay to return. Make sure the men understand that they need to negotiate this in advance of taking a time-out, at a time when both partners are calm.

There are three choices when reconnecting:

1. Drop the whole argument. It may not be worth the time or energy to continue to focus on the specific subject.

2. Agree to delay the discussion for a set amount of time while both people calm down and think things over.

3. Resume the discussion in a respectful manner.

Regardless of the choice, they will need to take another time-out if they sense they are beginning to escalate during reconnection.

Emphasize that the offer to reconnect needs to be respectful and ultimately is up to his partner. The length of their time-out can be from a couple of minutes to months or years, or perhaps never in a face-to-face encounter.

Emphasize the need to practice this time-out plan in small situations as well as big situations. The more the men practice, the less likely they will be abusive. Explain that they may have to return and leave several times, even after believing they have calmed down, to keep themselves from being abusive. Point out that it will be tempting to stay when they should take a time-out, and it will also be tempting to return too soon. Time-outs are difficult, but if the man doesn't take a time-out, it's only a matter of time before more abuse occurs.

In a follow-up session, have them read their time-out plan aloud. This gives them the opportunity to be accountable to the group. Ask if they have explained the plan to their partner (if they have one). Remind them that failure to do so can lead to further distrust and potential problems. After each man has shared his plan, have the group discuss the similarities in the plans. Discuss circumstances that require them to readjust the plans; for example, if their time-out contact person is unavailable. Emphasize the importance of sticking to the plan when they begin to feel they are escalating.

If you want to have the men monitor their use of the responsibility plan, direct them to the Responsibility Plan Monitoring Worksheet. We recommend you follow up on this worksheet as part of the weekly check-in. Give them the opportunity to share what they are learning about themselves by monitoring their own plan.

Issues

1. *Some men may minimize the need to do this activity.* Give these men the opportunity to explain why this activity isn't valuable. They often say, "I no longer have a partner," or "I only was abusive once and I won't be again." Discuss your view (and experience from working with other men) that the pattern of abuse will continue even with new partners if the men don't change their thoughts, attitudes, and habits. If they persist in stating that they do not need a plan, respond that this tells you they don't see their past behaviors as serious, and they probably will be abusive again. Discuss your program policy regarding nonparticipation.

2. *Let them know that a time-out does not solve any problems, but it does help them take care of themselves and reduce the risk of using abusive behaviors.* After the time-out, they can try to solve the specific problem. The plan itself is simply a tool for prevention and safety.

3. *Emphasize the benefits of the responsibility plan.* Lack of a plan indicates that they may continue to hold their partner responsible for keeping them from being abusive. Have the men discuss how their plans will help them. Point out that the plan is *not* a convenient way to get out of the house to be with friends; such use only decreases trust.

4. *Support them for remembering ways that they kept from being abusive in the past.* Let them know that times when they were not abusive are examples of times they chose not to be abusive. Thus, they can continue to make decisions that don't result in abuse.

5. *Driving, using drugs, drinking, or going to a bar are not recommended options for taking a time-out.* When they are upset, these activities could put their own or someone else's life in jeopardy. People often drive recklessly when they are angry. Drinking or using drugs may heighten one's potential for being abusive. Finally, going to a bar may give them the opportunity to abuse someone else, get abused themselves, or simply hang out with other people who are at the bar for the same reason.

6. *Some men refuse to leave an escalating situation under any circumstance.* Their reasons may be closely connected to the obstacles to leaving. All you can do as a counselor is talk about the high probability that they will be abusive if they stay in an escalating situation. Point out that refusing to leave not only contributes to the problem, but is a refusal to take care of themselves. If a man argues that his partner will break his belongings or call the police if he leaves, you can point out that this may happen if he stays, too. Help this man understand that the real reason for staying is his belief that staying gives him more control over the situation and ultimately, his partner. Seek profes-

sional input and support from other counselors in the field to discuss ways to deal with this type of client and to vent your frustrations and concerns.

7. *Some men have difficulty identifying methods of leaving in a positive way.* Some men state that they will just leave without speaking. This is acceptable only if their partner is aware of the responsibility plan and the goal of maintaining trust in the relationship. Explore how it feels and the messages it sends when a person just walks out in the middle of an argument. Discuss some of the fears a partner may face in such a situation. Discuss the importance of talking about this plan with their partners at a time when neither person is angry or upset.

8. *Their self-talk suggestions are often limited to not wanting to go to jail or return to jail.* There is nothing wrong with this motivation; it happens to be one of the first alternative self-talk statements these men will suggest. Support *whatever* self-talk it takes to leave an escalating situation. Explore other reasons to give themselves, such as, "I don't want to hurt someone I love," "I don't want my kids to hear this," "I can control myself," or "I need to take care of myself here."

9. *It is important that the men specify where they will go, what they will do, and about how long they will need to be gone during their time-out.* Some men resist committing themselves to anything concrete. Explain that the specifics help them account to themselves and the group. Note: Our suggestion of three options is a minimum amount; we believe men must have at least three alternatives, in case one or two fail.

10. *Encourage the men to record as many time-out contacts as possible, including family, friends, or group members.* Explain that these contact people do not need to solve the men's problems; they are people who will listen without making negative comments about the partner. Contact people also may be people they can spend time talking to about feelings or situations. Since group members can serve as contact people, prepare a phone list of men from the group who want to be available as contact people. If someone doesn't have a telephone, have them list their address to indicate that they are interested in being available. Distribute the list among those men who volunteered their names.

11. *Emphasize that they need to respect their partners' decisions about reconnecting.* A partner's choice to keep a man away rather than reconnecting does not necessarily mean the relationship is over; it could reflect her own need for more time-out. Explore how a man may feel when his partner makes some decisions he does not like. If a reconnection is not working, he may need to repeat his time-out plan.

12. *Some men are reluctant to share their plans with their partners.* Encourage them to share parts of the plan in shorter discussions if that makes them feel more comfortable. Reinforce that failure to inform their partner reduces trust in the relationship.

Notes, comments, and observations:

Participant's Workbook Sample

Goals

In this activity, you will:

1. Increase the use of nonabusive options when dealing with feelings that have led to the desire to control your partner.

2. Develop a plan with several options to stop yourself from escalating to abuse.

3. Develop a respectful plan to communicate with your partner or ex-partner.

4. Understand the obstacles to leaving an argument and develop some techniques to overcome those obstacles.

WORSHEET 12   Responsibility Plan

1. **Things to do to avoid becoming abusive**

   a. *Previous actions.* (Things you have done in the past to help yourself deal with your feelings in a nonabusive way.)

   b. *Obstacles to leaving.* (What beliefs or self-talk keep you from taking a time-out?)

   c. *Alternative self-talk.* (What positive things have you said to yourself to get past the obstacles?)

2. **The time-out plan**

   - What signals tell you that you need a time-out?

   - What will you do or say to leave in a positive way?

   - What will you say to yourself (positive self-talk) to help you leave?

   - Where will you go, what will you do, and how long will you be gone?
     Option A:
     Option B:
     Option C:

   - People you can contact who will help you cool down:
     Option A:
     Option B:
     Option C:

(continued)

WORKSHEET 12 (continued)

3. **The reconnecting plan**

   • What signals within yourself will tell you that you are ready to approach your partner in a respectful manner?

   • What can you do or say to reconnect in a way that is respectful of your partner and yourself?

   _____ *I have explained this plan to my current partner.*
   (date)

WORKSHEET 13   Responsibility Plan Monitoring Worksheet

Each time you use your plan in the next three weeks, record the following:

Date	What the situation was:	What you were thinking before the situation:	How you were feeling before the situation:	What you were thinking during the situation:	How you were feeling during the situation:	What you were thinking after the situation:	How you were feeling after the situation:

May Not Be Reproduced

Cluster 2

Steps toward Insight

Most Violent Behavior

Goals

In this activity, participants will:

1. Better understand how past abusive behaviors affect their relationships, other people, and themselves.

2. Talk specifically about their abusive behaviors, including what they did, how they felt, and what they were thinking.

3. Begin (or continue) the healing process in their life.

4. Deal directly with their feelings about their own behaviors.

5. Begin to take responsibility for their abusive behaviors.

6. Understand how to use insight gained from current and past behaviors to avoid being abusive in the future.

7. Reveal their attitudes about their behaviors to others and to themselves.

8. Describe their most violent behavior from their point of view.

Required Worksheet

My Most Violent Behavior (Worksheet 14)

Format

This is one of the most powerful sessions in the curriculum, as it requires the men to publicly acknowledge and talk about their abusive behavior. We have used two approaches with this activity; both are equally effective, but they serve separate purposes.

The first approach is to prepare the group for this activity at least one session in advance. Explain the purpose, goals, and process that will be used for the activity. This approach may increase the men's anxiety about the activity, giving them time to make up a story. However, it may benefit some men to experience this anxiety and may help others prepare to speak in a more organized presentation. It works best for men who need preparation and no surprises.

The second approach is to give no advance preparation for the session. This approach has the effect of catching the men off guard, at least for the first few who speak, resulting in a wealth of spontaneous and unedited thoughts. Its shortcoming is that the men's accounts tend to be longer and less organized. It works best for men who are likely to carefully guard their thoughts and need to be surprised to disclose information.

Regardless of the approach you choose, tell the group that this activity is one of the most difficult parts of the program because each man will have to talk about his most violent abuse of a partner (not necessarily a current partner). Explain that this disclosure will accomplish many goals. The men will:

- Break through the secrets that can be barriers to further growth.

- Get things out in the open in the group.

- Hear that they are not the only ones who have been abusive.

- Become aware of the similarities of the feelings men have about abuse.

- Begin or continue taking responsibility for their behaviors.

- Begin or enhance healing the pain they feel about their abusive behaviors.

- Begin changing specific unwanted behaviors—changes that can only occur when they identify the specific behaviors they want to change.

Ask the men to turn to the worksheet, My Most Violent Behavior. Explain that they will be asked to talk specifically about a situation in which they were the most abusive or violent with a partner. The situation may be recent or from a long time ago. The partner may be a current or former partner. The type of violence may not have been physical, but the behavior must be the most abusive from the man's perspective. Advise the men to be honest, and use "I" statements when describing the situation. This will help them avoid blaming their partner for the abuse. Also, point out that they could fool the group by inventing a story, and no one would know the difference—but that this is a time for self-honesty and risk taking. Ask, "What do you have to lose by telling the truth?"

Read through the exercise with the men. It includes these questions:

- Describe your most violent situation.

- What was happening before you were abusive?

- What, specifically, was the argument about?

- What exact names, words, or actions did you use?

- How long did this situation escalate?

- What were your signals? What were you thinking? Feeling?

- What abuse did you do?

- While being abusive, what were you thinking? Feeling?

- What did you do after you were abusive?

- After you were abusive, what were you thinking? Feeling?

Explain that you will need a volunteer to tell his story. While the volunteer speaks, no one may interrupt him except you, whose job is to clarify his story, keep him on time and on track, and help him avoid blaming his partner. Explain that after the man has described his situation, the group will have time to respond. This feedback should be limited to questions or comments related to the situation described. Remind the men to use "I" statements, not "shoulds," when giving feedback.

Discuss any time limitations or constraints. Be open to their questions about the purpose of the exercise, and provide more explanation if needed.

There are a variety of ways to carry out this exercise. We have used three variations, presented below. Please feel free to combine them or come up with your own that fits for your style of counseling.

Option One   Ask the men to turn to the My Most Violent Behavior worksheet. Give them fifteen to twenty minutes to complete the first page. Let them know that each of them will be sharing their accounts in the large group. When you reassemble, ask for a volunteer to begin. Have him read or describe the situation. Have him explain his pattern of being abusive during the situation. Repeat this process until everyone has participated.

Option Two   Distribute blank pieces of paper and crayons, markers, pencils, or pens. Explain that they will have fifteen to twenty minutes to draw or symbolize their most violent situation and their pattern of being abusive. Let them know that they will be explaining these drawings to the group. As the first volunteer talks about his picture and his situation, ask him to refer back to his picture. Let the picture become a reference point. Repeat this process until all members have shared.

Option Three   Write the outline of what you want them to talk about on the chalkboard. Conduct the exercise orally.

Throughout these options, consider asking some of the following questions, either of yourself, of the man speaking, or of the group:

- Is he talking about his feelings and thoughts?

- Is he clearly describing his abuse? Is he denying or minimizing?

- What was he trying to control in the situation? Was he successful?

- To what extent does he believe "she got what she deserved?"

- What gave him "permission" to abuse her in this situation? (That is, identify his self-talk or feelings.)

- Does he acknowledge or understand his partner's fear of him?

- Is he stating that he was "out of control" during the situation?

- How much responsibility for his actions and behaviors is he taking?

- What was his goal in being abusive—what did he want to happen?

- To what extent does he blame his drinking or other drug use for being violent?

Other things to listen for and respond to:

- Blaming his partner, the system, or others for the situation and his behavior, or otherwise refusing to take responsibility for his own actions.

- Minimizing his actions, his impact on his partner, or the effects of his control or power in the situation.

- Subtle and overt ways he continues to abuse or tries to control her.

- Rambling or talking about issues that are not pertinent to his most violent behaviors.

Provide observations and questions during the time the other group members give feedback to the speaker. Focus on the man's behavior, not on his partner or the system. After each person has given feedback on the man's situation, highlight some of the positive comments and summarize any concerns you have for that individual. Give him the "final word," in which he may speak directly to individuals within the group, the counselor, or the group as a whole. He can use this time without interruptions from anyone, including the counselor, to address disagreements or confirmations of what he heard from others.

Finally, thank him for sharing his story, reassert how risky the exercise was for him, and emphasize the positive aspects of his story. For example, focus on when a man sincerely takes responsibility for any or all of his behaviors. Be respectful of this process—men feel vulnerable during this exercise. Balance your confrontational interventions with supportive ones.

After everyone has shared, discuss the impact this exercise has had on the group. Discuss how it felt to talk about their abusive behavior, and how it feels now that they have completed this part of the program. Discuss what they have gained, lost, or learned. Talk with them about the difficulties in doing this exercise.

Finally, if you are using Option One, discuss the rest of the worksheet—the sections on how the abuse affected them, their relationships, and other people. Explain that they will need to complete the rest of the worksheet and be prepared to talk about their responses during a follow-up session.

We recommend that you end this session with a positive self-statement or a way the men can nurture themselves during the next week.

Follow-Up

During the next session, discuss the remainder of the worksheet. (If you chose Option One, you can follow the worksheet itself. For Options Two or Three, proceed orally, following the basic format of the worksheet.) Have each member share his responses to the remaining questions, and keep him on track using the same questions and tips we suggested on pages 82-83. Remind the group of the philosophical principles when appropriate. Discuss how this activity has been helpful to them. Give the men credit for the work that they have done for themselves in this process.

Issues

1. *A key element to this exercise is your individual relationship with the speaker.* In most cases he has already told you his most violent behavior. If you keep notes, review them and be prepared to subtly and respectfully guide or redirect the man as he shares his situation and behaviors with the group. You may also have access to the police report or a presentence investigation. This is particularly useful should a group member state that he has never been abusive. Give each man the opportunity to bring out his story, even if he's not totally accurate according to these other sources. You can come back later to some of the important details.

2. *When you have told the group what the activity is, there will be a variety of reactions.* Observe the body language of the group members. Some men may look defensive, some may appear ashamed, and some may seem uncertain, but anticipatory. The mere mention of violence and their behavior in the same sentence will elicit a number of signals for you to observe. To reassure the men, clarify and explain the activity; you may need to repeat your explanation even after several men have shared.

3. *Some men refuse to do the activity.* Give them an opportunity to explain their reasons. Some common reasons: "I want to put it behind me," "I don't want to dig up things from the past," "I have already talked about this to others," "I have already dealt with what I've done, now I need

to move on," "I get too angry when I think of that stuff, so I've just forgotten it." Have these men identify their feelings and concerns about doing this exercise. Acknowledge those feelings and concerns, but explain the participation policy or expectations the group discussed and agreed upon in the first session. Avoid a power struggle at the early stages of this activity. Some of this reaction may be related to being fearful. State your expectations and move on to further clarification of the exercise. Often the men who initially refuse will participate when they see others participate.

4. *After two or three men have taken their turn, discuss how everyone feels.* Men who have talked about their violent behavior can relate how it feels to get it out in the open and get it over with. This relieves some of the tension, and encourages those men who have been afraid to tell their story.

5. *The last group member to share may insistently refuse to do this activity.* Before you remind him of the participation policy, ask the group to talk about how it felt to tell their story, what they expected, and how they felt afterward. If the man stays firm in his refusal, ask the group about how they would feel if the man continued in the group without at least attempting to tell his story. Expect responses such as distrust, anger, and concern that he won't complete the group. Remember, group pressure is usually more effective than laying down the law—although ultimately, you may need to do so. When you do get into this position, make your statements clear and your expectations concrete. Seek professional input and supervisory support when dealing with these situations. Don't back into a corner or make a decision on the spur of the moment.

6. *The focus of the exercise is the man's behavior toward a partner or ex-partner.* On occasion a man may feel that his most abusive behavior was towards his mother, a sister or brother, his father, or a child. If you are aware from individual counseling sessions of his abusive behaviors toward a partner, redirect his focus on this relationship for this exercise. It may be helpful at some point to discuss this man's abusive behavior toward others. In these cases, point out that in each case, abuse helped the man keep or seek power and control over another person.

7. *Often, men get sidetracked or begin to place the responsibility for their behaviors on other people.* Respectfully redirect their attention by reminding them that the focus is on their behavior, not other people's behavior. Use some of the questions on pages 82-83 in the format section to redirect the man's story.

8. *Remember that you can only ask questions, probe the situation, provide observations, and state how much responsibility this person takes for his actions.* Trying to change his attitudes during this activity will only frustrate you and the group. Avoid power struggles. Draw observations and concerns from the other group members. A man who takes little or no responsibility for his actions needs to clearly hear your concern that he is minimizing or denying his abusive behaviors and that as long as he does so, he is at risk for repeating the abuse.

9. *You need to make a policy decision about whether participation in this session is essential to completing the program.* If this exercise is essential to completing the program, have a plan in place for dealing with those men who refuse to participate. This may include consulting with the probation officer, court worker, your supervisor, or colleagues.

10. *Be alert for a man who describes his situation, begins to escalate, and seems to suggest that he could or would repeat his abusive actions.* Warning signs include: minimizing or denying the effects of his abuse; an attitude that his partner deserved to be abused; and statements that when he sees his partner again he just gets madder and madder. These signs are cause for your concern for the safety of his partner. Ask other group members if they can corroborate your concern. Be aware of the state, local, and federal laws regarding a counselor's duty to warn the authorities or a potential victim of imminent danger. Consult your supervisor or colleagues for input and support as needed.

11. *Sometimes a man states that he has never been abusive and has no idea why he is in the group.* Draw on the information you have gathered from this man's individual sessions. Within the group, explore his concept of violence and abuse. Tell the man that from all the evidence you've seen, he did indeed abuse his partner. Explain that you are concerned that since he can't admit he was abusive, he will probably continue to abuse people, and this is most likely not the end or even the worst of it. Tell him that he needs to think seriously about his choices, and if he chooses not to deal with his abusive behaviors, it doesn't make much sense for him to continue in the group. Tell him that you will discuss with your supervisor whether he should remain in the program, since it appears he won't benefit from it. Note that you may also need to talk with his partner, probation officer, court worker, and others who have evidence of his abuse and who may be affected by his release from the domestic abuse program.

12. *Some men claim their drug use or drinking caused them to be abusive.* Acknowledge that chemicals can be a factor in abuse. Then explore any other feelings these men had before they started using or drinking, as well as the thoughts and feelings they had while using chemicals. Some men state they blacked out or can't remember what they did. Ask them

to talk about what other people (partner, police, probation officer, judge) said he did. Ask if chemical use is a justification for abuse. Be clear that drugs or alcohol do not cause abuse. Remind such men of the program principle of being responsible for one's own actions. Discuss the risk of future danger to themselves or others if they black out and become violent again. Inform him if you need to warn authorities or potential victims. Refer clients to chemical dependency assessment or treatment, Alcoholics Anonymous, Narcotics Anonymous, or other support group as appropriate.

13. *Sometimes a man states that he was out of control and "just reacted."* We use four challenges to help such a man recognize that he really was in control of himself. The challenges are:

A. He was not there and did not commit any abuse. If so, how was he accused and sentenced for an action he did not commit?

B. He was crazy, out of his mind, or unable to control his actions. Refute this assertion by asking the following questions, which should help you show how much self-control he actually had. These questions are applicable even if the man attributes his behavior to drugs or drinking.

   - Could he have injured his partner more seriously? Why didn't he?

   - Who is the usual target of his abuse? Does he abuse his employers? Friends? Acquaintances? Why not? Did he hit or threaten to hit someone else?

   - At what point did he come to his senses and begin to make, in his mind, rational decisions again? Did anyone intervene?

   - Why was the abuse at home or in an isolated area and not in the street or in a public place?

C. He just reacted: It was a reflex and he had no time to think. Review the concepts of signals, patterns of abuse, and his escalation process during the situation. Ask if escalation is the way he "just reacts" to certain situations and if so, is he dangerous to the general public? When something like this happens again, will he act abusively? If not, what makes him think he won't act abusively? If he states "that's just the way things are," explore whether he likes to be abusive and if things have to stay the same.

D. If he committed the abuse, wasn't crazy, and didn't really "just react," then the only remaining explanation is that he actually did have control of himself. Discuss the logic of this argument and feel satisfied if he only begins to understand that he had control. You've made progress if a man says he *feels* like he was out of control but recognizes that ultimately he made a decision to be abusive. Avoid power struggles.

14. *It is important for the man to be very specific about the words he used, the signals that pushed his buttons and his abusive behaviors.* Often, men will generalize the situation, which allows them to minimize their feelings, abuse, and impact on others. The man who minimizes this way may not recognize it until someone points it out. Continue to redirect him to specific words, signals, and behaviors. Also, guide his language about his partner and the situation; statements like "It was just a spat," or "She gets that way" indicate that he is minimizing his behaviors.

15. *For many of the men, the alternative to minimizing or denying their abusive behaviors is total vulnerability and shame.* Remember, you are dealing with some psychic wounds. Be respectful of their healing process. Due to their shame, the most you may be able to do is let them know you like them (if you do) or that nothing is wrong with them as a human being, but what they did was unacceptable and must stop. Give them credit for whatever they share; even if it's only a little, it is a start. Your concerns or observations will make a big impact on these men, as will your avoidance of power struggles, which models the new behavior you are trying to teach. You must hold them accountable for their behavior by continuing to challenge their negative actions and destructive decisions, and by supporting positive alternatives.

16. *Often, a man will have difficulty identifying the effects of his abusive behavior on others.* During his description, he tends to see the situation as an isolated incident. Discuss with the group the fear the partner must feel during and after the abuse. Explore the man's own fears during the situation. Examine the differences between his fears and his partner's fears. Discuss whether there was *any* abuse that happened before this or since. Discuss the effects on the children. Even though the children may not have been present, what might they have sensed? Another way to address this is by asking the man to reflect on his experiences in his own family of origin. If he came from a violent home, what does he remember? How did it feel?

17. *Sometimes a man states that his partner deserved the abuse.* Explore his justification for abusing anyone, especially someone he loves. Discuss if it is okay for others to abuse him. Point out his double standards and have the group talk about them. Discuss how a man has to objectify another person (think of a person as a thing or belonging) in order to abuse that person. Explore his thinking and the reasons he gave himself for being abusive. Relate this to his partner's ongoing fear due to emotional abuse or other types of abuse. Examine his degree of empathy for his partner. Ask the other group members how they would feel in the situation. If the man continues to believe that his partner deserved to be abused, you will need to clearly state your concern that he will repeat the abuse.

18. *After a man describes his most violent behavior, tell him about his tone of voice and body language while speaking.* This helps the man get an objective view of his behaviors. Ask other group members to talk about what they perceived. Ask the man if his feelings match the group's observations. Discuss with the group how they would feel as this man's partner, seeing and hearing him describe the situation.

19. *The follow-up questions on the worksheet are extremely important.* After the men complete the first part of this exercise, they generally seem to feel cohesive as a group. They have shared some dark secrets with each other and have attained a higher level of mutual trust. This feeling can be strong and they may think that this is the end of the program. In order to maintain some intensity and encourage them to see the impact of their behaviors, the follow-up questions are essential. You usually will be in a better position to challenge them further when discussing their responses to these questions after completing the first part of this activity. Respectfully discuss and examine their answers. Probe beyond their written or quick easy answers. Use group interventions as much as possible.

20. *Talk with the group about ways to nurture themselves after these group sessions.* Suggest going out for coffee after meetings, calling each other, being alone, going out with someone else, or whatever it takes. The feelings that come up during this exercise can be overwhelming.

21. *Look for ways to take care of yourself.* This is a stressful work situation in the first place. The situations and abuse you hear about in this exercise will compound the stress. Seek some professional and personal nurturing during the times you are leading this group, but especially during these sessions. Give yourself a break. An overstressed and emotionally unavailable counselor will not be as effective or efficient. Clients deserve a mentally healthy counselor.

22. *Some men seem incapable of change, and this can be very frustrating for you.* Review your expectations for the group and the individuals. Reevaluate and alter them appropriately. Seek support from supervisors or others in the field. A great deal of frustration occurs when someone doesn't change their attitudes as fast or as far as we would like, or does not seem to understand the application of the information or exercise.

23. *Be aware of how powerful this exercise can be.* Provide resources for other counseling or support when necessary. This activity will affect them and you. Be mindful of your professional and personal processes and boundaries. Get professional support and input whenever possible. Continue to sharpen your skills and improve your counseling by listening to the clients.

Notes, comments, and observations:

Participant's Workbook Sample

Goals

In this activity, you will:

1. Better understand how your past abusive behaviors affect your relationships, other people, and yourself.

2. Talk specifically about your abusive behaviors, including what you did, how you felt, and what you were thinking.

3. Begin (or continue) the healing process in your life.

4. Deal directly with your feelings about your own behaviors.

5. Begin to take responsibility for your abusive behaviors.

6. Understand how to use what you've learned about your current and past behaviors to avoid being abusive in the future.

7. Reveal your attitudes about your behaviors to other members of the group—and to yourself.

8. Describe your most violent behavior from your point of view.

WORSHEET 14   My Most Violent Behavior

Describe the situation in which you were the most abusive with a spouse, significant other, or partner. Include what happened before the situation began. What specifically did you argue about? What sort of names or words were used? How long ago did this happen?

Identify your pattern of being abusive during this situation:

- Your signals and escalation:

- What you were thinking:

- What you were feeling:

- What abuse you committed:

- What injuries your partner received:

- What you were thinking as you were being abusive:

- What you were feeling as you were being abusive:

- What happened after you were abusive:

- What you were thinking after you were abusive:

- How you felt after you were abusive: **(continued)**

WORKSHEET 14 (continued)

Follow-up questions

How do you feel when you think about what you did to her?

In what ways did your abusive behavior in this situation affect you:

- physically (for example, did your hand hurt, or did you have a hangover?)
- socially
- intellectually
- spiritually
- emotionally
- sexually

In what ways did your abusive behavior in this situation affect the relationship:

- physically
- socially
- intellectually
- spiritually
- emotionally
- sexually

In what ways did your abusive behavior in this situation affect others (family, children)?

What have you gained in the relationship by doing these abusive behaviors?

What have you lost?

What will you need to do to gain support for who you are as a person?

What specific behaviors will you need to change in this relationship because of the abusive actions you used with your partner?

What changes do you need to make (or have you already made) that might restore this relationship? Does your partner want to restore the relationship?

What are you not able to change?

When she brings up the subject of your abusive behavior, how will you feel? What self-talk will you need to use? How can you respond in a positive, nonviolent manner?

What have you learned about your behavior and yourself from this situation?

Goals

In this activity, participants will:

1. Better understand what control is.

2. Identify the methods they have used to control others.

3. Better understand that the only person one can control is oneself.

4. Develop a control monitoring system to help them practice alternatives to controlling people.

5. Develop a self-control support network.

Control Strategies (Worksheet 15)
Control Monitoring System (Worksheet 16)

To prepare the men for this activity, discuss their definitions of control. Talk about control from as many angles as possible, including control of a car; control of one's feelings, actions, and thoughts; control of one's environment; and the differences between controlling and influencing.

Direct the discussion to the question of who they can ultimately control. Ask if they have ever been controlled by someone and if so, to what extent. Ask if they had choices even though they felt like someone controlled them.

Explore the concept of control by discussing a situation that parallels the client's situation: an intervention with a chemically dependent person. Describe how such an intervention works, and then ask some of the following questions:

- What are the intentions of someone who tries to get a person to go to drug treatment, even though the person does not want to go?

- Does the positive intent (coercing a person into treatment so he or she stays alive) outweigh or justify the approach used in the intervention?

- How does a well-meaning person try to "force" someone to be healthy?

- Ultimately, who decides whether a person stops drinking or using drugs?

Such a person may reach a point where drug use means death. The choices are few, but there is still a choice; the person may choose to use drugs knowing that he will die. The choice to use is still his. Ultimately, *the power of choice lies in the hands of the one who must make that choice.* The only person one can control is oneself. Discuss other aspects of control as they relate to the eight principles of this program. For example, often men do not abuse people such as employers or good friends; how are these men able to control themselves in these relationships and not with their partners?

Ask the men to turn to Worksheet 15, Control Strategies. Give the men a few minutes to write their personal definition of control. Ask each member to read his definition aloud. List key phrases from each definition on the chalkboard.

Give the group fifteen minutes to complete the rest of the worksheet. (Another option: assign the worksheet as homework and discuss it in a follow-up session.)

During the follow-up discussion of the worksheet, ask each member specifically who they tried to control and the strategies they used. When each man has responded, ask some of the following questions:

- How are the control strategies similar?

- What is similar about whom the men chose to control?

- Which strategies were easiest to use?

- How did the men decide which strategy to use in a given situation?

- How might their awareness of their controlling strategies help them be less abusive in the future?

- What things, situations, or people can't they control?

- What do they gain from trying to control others? What are their rewards for controlling others?

Have the group brainstorm rewards and gains for letting go of trying to control others.

Help the group talk about the grief and feelings of loss over not trying to control others. Discuss their responses to the worksheet question, "It hurts when you realize you can't control others. How can you address the feelings of loss for not being able to control people or situations?" Let them know that these feelings are normal.

Discuss what each group member *can* control in his life. Within the group, develop a list of people to contact and places to go to nurture self-control. Help the group members identify and develop alternative strategies to controlling others. Explain that the strategies must be practiced in order to stop abuse; this kind of change is a long process.

Have each member commit to using their alternative strategies during a specified time period. During the remaining weeks, ask each member to discuss their progress with their alternative strategies.

You may suggest the men use the Control Monitoring System to help them pay closer attention to this issue. Suggest that for one week they keep track of situations in which they felt they had to "take control." Emphasize that they make brief, concise notes. Review the log after one week. If the men have not filled out the log, give them the first ten minutes of the next session to fill in one or two situations from the previous week.

Issues

1. *Many men say that there are times they are not in control of themselves.* Have them describe a particular time when they felt they were out of control. Then ask them to state at least two alternatives to the actions they took. Accept that they may feel out of control, but explain that feelings are different from actions. Since there were clearly alternatives to the actions they took, they made a choice to be controlling. It may have been the only choice they felt they could make, but they were in control—and now that they have many alternatives, they can pick one that is not abusive. Review the Program Principles related to self-control (page 39).

2. *Some men don't understand that they have tried to control people, and so may be unable to think of a person they have tried to control.* Discuss their definitions of control and subtle strategies of control. If they still can't think of anyone, have them choose a behavior from their most violent behavior activity. Ask them who the violent behavior was against. Then have them complete the worksheet with that situation and person in mind.

3. *Grief and loss are feelings that are not often explored with men who have been abusive.* Do not avoid these feelings. Talk about how some men have developed positive, healthy ways to express these feelings when they have let go of trying to control others, such as crying, or developing a ritual or celebration to put closure on the feelings of grief. Explain that they may decide to avoid their grief by controlling others.

4. *Alternative strategies are meant to be positive ways of growing beyond the feelings of loss and hurt.* The larger goal is to help these men develop positive ways to take care of themselves, rather than trying to control someone or something else. Trying to control someone else is a setup for failure in that it is frustrating and diverts them from taking care of themselves.

5. *Discuss the meaning of "letting go."* The concept is common in therapy and among people involved in various recovery programs, but it will be

new to most of these men. It is essential to this activity. Help them identify specific ways they can "let go" of someone else. For example they can use self-talk messages such as:

- What or who can I control here?

- Am I taking care of myself by doing this?

- Am I setting myself up for disappointment because this person is going to do what they want no matter what I do?

- How can I "let go" in this situation?

Discuss ways that they have already let go of some things or people in their lives.

6. *Encourage the group members to list three or four people they can talk to or places they can get support for not controlling others.* Explain that the lack of support or nurturing for such change could affect whether they will continue to control others.

7. *The alternative strategies should be simple and specific.* Many men may make general strategy statements. The more general the statements are, the less the men really commit to changing. At the other end, some men may make too many elaborate commitments. If they develop overly complex alternative strategies, they may become frustrated and give up on the plan.

8. *Expect some resistance to developing these strategies.* These strategies are change-oriented; it is safer and more comfortable to keep old behaviors. You can overcome some of this resistance by helping the men see the value and benefits of change. Continue to discuss the pros and cons of staying the same. Ask some questions such as, "Do you like the way things are now? Are you willing to put in some extra effort to try something new? How do others view your behavior?"

Notes, comments, and observations:

Participant's Workbook Sample

Goals

In this activity, you will:

1. Better understand what control is.

2. Identify the methods you have used to control others.

3. Better understand that the only person you can control is yourself.

4. Develop a control monitoring system to help you practice alternatives to controlling people.

5. Develop a self-control support network.

WORKSHEET 15 — Control Strategies

1. What does the word "control" mean to you?

2. Names of people you have tried to control:

   a.

   b.

   c.

   d.

3. What you have done to try to control others:

   a.

   b.

   c.

4. What people, things, or situations can't you control in your life?

5. What do you gain by trying to control these people or things?

6. What do you gain by "letting go" of trying to control others?

   a.

   b.

   c.

7. It hurts when you realize you can't control others. How can you address the feelings of loss for not being able to control people or situations?

(continued)

WORKSHEET 15 (continued)

8. What *can* you control in your life?

   a.

   b.

   c.

9. Who will support your efforts to focus on the things you can control in your life? Where can you go to get support for those efforts?

10. List some nonviolent alternatives you can use when you realize you are trying to control another person:

    a.

    b.

    c.

WORKSHEET 16   Control Monitoring System

Date	Situation	People involved	Your feelings	What you wanted to control	What you did to get control	Alternative strategies for future situations

May Not Be Reproduced

Goals

In this activity, participants will:

1. Define male privilege.

2. Understand the role of male privilege in society and in relationships with partners.

3. Recognize the rewards and consequences of male privilege.

4. Develop some alternatives to the use of male privilege.

Male Privilege (Worksheet 17)

Ask the men to turn to the Male Privilege worksheet. Ask the group to define the word "power." Record their responses on the chalkboard, and tell them to record the responses on their worksheet as well. Discuss the definitions on the board. Repeat the process with the term "privilege." Discuss the similarities and differences in the two terms.

Ask the men to form groups of three to five members. Give the groups ten minutes to list examples of male privilege in our society. Then have the small groups come together and record their lists on the chalkboard and on their worksheets.

Now that the men have explored the meanings of male power and male privilege, you can offer your interpretation. Before the group session in which you use this activity, write the definition of male privilege on a large piece of cardboard. We use the following definition to begin the discussion:

Male Privilege

Male privilege consists of rights, powers, exemptions, and advantages given to men by men. Men control these rights and monitor them. Men grant and remove these rights from women and children. This granting and removal of privileges keeps women and children constantly off-balance, constantly in search of power, and constantly in fear. In this way, men control the behavior of women and children. *Ultimately, men retain their privilege by keeping women and children dependent on men for food, shelter, safety, emotional stability, and the money to obtain these basic human needs.*

Also before this activity, write out the operating principles of male privilege. We have listed twelve principles as follows:

The Twelve Operating Principles of Privilege

1. Privileged people don't have to follow the rules they set up.

2. Unprivileged people aren't as valuable as privileged people.

3. Unprivileged people should do undesirable work for the privileged.

4. Privileged people have the right to interpret, educate, and otherwise tell the unprivileged how to view the world and the laws.

5. The privileged define intelligence for the unprivileged. The unprivileged are only considered "intelligent" when the privileged can recognize their ways of knowing and understanding. In other words, unprivileged people's different ways of knowing have no value.

6. It is the responsibility of the privileged to measure and evaluate unprivileged people's learning in accordance and compliance with the understanding of the privileged.

7. Unprivileged people have value only in relation to the privileged and the people who act like them.

8. Privileged people set their own limits and can extend them as far as they wish. Unprivileged people can't stop them.

9. Only the privileged can criticize their own system. Anyone else will suffer consequences for doing so, and only the privileged can determine those consequences.

10. Unprivileged people are not allowed direct or honest communication with the privileged.

11. The privileged control communication and decide what kind of communication is relevant.

12. Any breakdowns or challenges to the system are caused by the unprivileged, not the privileged.

To help the men understand the definition and principles, discuss the principles as if the source of privilege is race (white) and not gender (male). Help them realize that the only fact that changes is who benefits and who suffers. Otherwise the content is the same. Discuss some similarities of racism and sexism. You can apply the same principles to age, wealth, class, or other forms of privilege.

After this discussion, give the men ten minutes to fill in the "power chart" on their worksheet, answering the question, "How do you get power physically, emotionally, intellectually, spiritually, socially?" Discuss how each group member affects others through his male privilege. The discussion can be generalized to the overall effects of male privilege, or specific to how each man sees his male privilege affecting other people.

Discuss and explain the continuum of male privilege and attitudes about it. Explain that all men lie on this continuum. (See Figure A, below.)

⬅————————————————➡	
Unbiased attitude and behavior toward women	*Total objectification of women; degradation and killing of women*

Figure A

Some men are on the far extreme of the continuum. Their behavior includes killing women, sexually degrading them, or committing serial crimes against them. Men in the middle of the continuum exhibit blatantly sexist attitudes or negative behaviors toward women. Men at the other end of this continuum behave in a manner consistent with the belief that men and women are equal. These men are aware of their own biases and social biases about women, and are willing to behave differently from these biases. Emphasize that all men are on this continuum, and when a man acts in some way that contributes to negative attitudes toward women, all men gain more power, even those who are far to the "unbiased" end of the continuum. Discuss how they use their male power in a relationship and ultimately what they would gain and lose by using it.

Brainstorm advantages of maintaining male privilege in a relationship. Identify what can be gained by letting go of this power. Discuss also what may be lost by letting go of the power; in other words, what is the worst that could happen if the men relinquish their male privilege? Help the group members develop ways of getting their needs met when grieving the loss of privilege.

Finally, discuss the meaning of empowerment and its differences from being powerful. Brainstorm a list of how and where they can become empowered. Ultimately, you hope to define empowerment as a state in which the individual feels capable to make choices that benefit him or her on all levels of being. Such power can't be given to anyone—that is, the counselor can't "empower" the client. It develops from within and is enhanced as both positive and negative choices are integrated in one's life.

Issues

1. *Male privilege will be difficult for some of the men to accept as true.* Most men who are court-ordered to a program feel that they are the *last* ones to have any privilege or power. Help them identify ways that men have advantages over women. Some examples would be: at work, on the street at night, at a bar, in business, in politics, and so forth. Ask the men if they feel safe. Ask how many of them think they might get raped by a woman. Allow them to talk about their views regarding power even if those views conflict with yours. Discuss the differences between use of power and abuse of power.

2. *The men will resist this activity.* Initially, they may react defensively and with great disbelief. Identifying, defining, and explaining the accumulation of power will help decrease their resistance. As you model how to talk about power and privilege, the men will lower their defenses.

3. *Use racism or ageism as a way to help the men understand sexism.* Some men quickly grasp the connection between these concepts. Encourage these men to explain the connections in their own words, as they will help the others understand. If there are people from a variety of cultures, draw on their personal experiences. Discuss white privilege in the United States, and relate this concept to the discussion of male privilege.

4. *This is an opportunity to challenge the men to grow in their understanding of others.* The object of this activity is to encourage the men to see themselves from another perspective. Some men will never understand your point. This can be frustrating, especially if you are in the latter stages of your program. Regardless, the exposure to *how* you handle this difficult discussion of power and privilege is invaluable to all group members. Avoid power struggles by offering your observations of how group members handle the topic of male privilege.

5. *Male privilege can be directly related to the activity, Men's Rules about Men.* Review this activity with the group. Discuss how men's rules about men and about women affect women.

6. *The question of why women stay in abusive relationships may be raised during this discussion, if it has not already been discussed.* Write the phrase "Why do women stay?" on the chalkboard. Under this question write and explain that some men say women stay because they like getting hurt, they are crazy, or they are stupid. Have the group brainstorm a list of reasons why women stay. Their responses may include: money, family, kids, religion, fear, love, no place to go, they feel powerless, they believe their partner will change, and so forth.

   Repeat the question, "Why do women stay?" and emphasize all the listed reasons. Then erase the "Wo" in women and ask the question "Why do men stay?" Erase the responses "they like it," "they are crazy," and "they are stupid." Explain your view that none of the men in the group are crazy, stupid, or like being abused, but that the remainder of the list would apply to men. Thus, you can shift the focus from the woman's responsibility to the man's responsibility in the relationship. This small exercise can be powerful because it is hard to argue against these human reasons for staying in a relationship. Give the group time to discuss this activity before moving back to the general discussion of power and male privilege. To connect to the main theme of power and privilege, ask some of the following questions: How is the question, "Why do women stay" itself an example of male privilege? What is the underlying message when men focus on the reasons women stay in abusive relationships rather than their responsibility for perpetrating abuse? How does this focus reflect different standards for men and women? Who sets the standards generally, in this society?

After discussing the term "empowerment," the group members need to hear your view on male privilege. Don't invite them to try to change your mind as a way to discuss this subject. Simply tell them your perspective. Trying to convince them to take on your values will just frustrate everyone.

7. *You must have a firm understanding of male privilege before conducting this activity.* Uncertainty on your part will weaken the exercise. Before presenting this activity, discuss male privilege with other professionals. Seek professional support and consultation to develop your philosophical framework for this activity.

Notes, comments, and observations:

Participant's Workbook Sample

Goals

In this activity, you will:

1. Define male privilege.

2. Understand the role of male privilege in society and in relationships with partners.

3. Recognize the rewards and consequences of male privilege

4. Develop some alternatives to the use of male privilege.

WORKSHEET 17   Male Privilege

1. What does power mean?

2. How is male privilege demonstrated in our society?

3. How do you get power?

Physically	Emotionally	Intellectually	Spiritually	Socially

4. How does your male privilege in society affect others?

5. What do you gain from maintaining your privilege as a male in society?

6. What sort of privileges do you have as a man in this society?

7. In what ways does a man have more power than a woman in a relationship?

8. What do you gain from maintaining your power as a male in your relationship?

9. What will you gain by sharing or letting go of this power?

10. What will you lose by sharing or letting go of this power?

11. How can you support yourself when grieving over this loss of power?

12. How and where can you become empowered?

May Not Be Reproduced

Goals

In this activity, participants will:

1. Better understand how their family of origin affects their behavior, particularly abusive behavior.

2. Understand that while their family of origin experiences may have influenced their decision to be violent, they are nevertheless responsible for their abusive actions.

3. Understand the messages they received as a child that modeled abusive ways of solving problems.

4. Better understand those experiences that affected their feelings, thoughts and behaviors while growing up.

5. Become more aware of attitudes they were exposed to as a child that carry over into adulthood, particularly attitudes about women.

Required Worksheets

Family Tree (Worksheet 18)
Family of Origin (Worksheet 19)

Format

◆◆◆

Ask the men to turn to their Family Tree worksheet. Break them into small groups. Ask them to draw their family tree, going back as far as they can. Be sure they include siblings, aunts and uncles, cousins, and grandparents. Also ask them to include divorces, stepparents, and stepsiblings, as well as notes on any deaths. Let the men use their own symbols and format for depicting their family. As they work, they should discuss their drawings within their small group. Give them twenty minutes to complete their drawings.

Reassemble the large group. Ask each member to talk about his family and where he fits within it. As each man describes his family tree, ask questions such as the following:

• Who were you closest to in the family?

• What was your relationship like with your mother and father?

• What did it feel like being firstborn (second, third, and so forth)?

• What did it feel like to be one child among so many kids? (Or, what did it feel like to be the only child?)

- What would have been more helpful to you growing up in this family?

- What are your relationships like with your family members now?

After everyone has shared their family tree, discuss the similarities and differences. Examine what the men can learn from listening to each other's family background. Ask, "How does it feel to hear about other families?" "What do you gain from hearing another man's story?"

Ask the men to turn to Worksheet 19, Family of Origin. Give them twenty minutes to respond to the questions on the worksheet. Explain that they will share some of their responses.

When the group reassembles, have a general discussion of their responses to these questions. Focus on obtaining information from as many group members as possible. Ask each man about his parent's relationship. Ask how they were disciplined as children and how that discipline felt. Discuss house rules and what rules were focused on. Ask what their school experience was like.

Talk about where and with what people they felt safe. Ask who they looked up to, whether in real life or in books, comics, movies, or television. Also, discuss the different expectations of boys and girls in the family, particularly around sex. Talk about family messages about what a man should be.

Next, discuss how these messages have affected their behavior. Have the group members discuss how and from whom they learned that violence and abuse were a way to cope with problems. Ask them to list these people on their worksheet. Discuss what attitudes and behaviors they learned from others and what they can do to change these attitudes and behaviors. Remind them that they do not always have to stay the same, even though their environment may be the same, and that as they change, other people will have to change their views and expectations of them. Discuss how they take responsibility for their own behaviors.

Finally, help them identify specific issues they may want to deal with in individual counseling, such as having been abused or having witnessed abuse. Be prepared to provide appropriate referrals as necessary. Reinforce how important it is for them to continue to think about the influence of their family of origin on their current behavior. As they increase their understanding of the effects of their past experience on their present beliefs, they will be better able to understand and control their behavior.

◆◆◆

Issues   1. *Family of origin is usually a very sensitive area.* Before you begin, explain the process to the men and tell them they are free to share as much or as little as they need to. As the activity progresses, ask the men how they feel and what they can do to support each other in coping with these issues, some of which they may never have thought about before. Suggest other resources for support in the community. Be prepared to provide resources that address these specific issues. Research the resources in your region before facilitating this discussion. Some men within the group may already have resources that they have used and found helpful, and which they may be willing to share with the group.

2. *This may be the first time some men have ever looked at their family of origin issues.* Be sensitive to these particular group members. Let them set the pace for how much and when they reveal information, and don't try to force insight on them. Let the men know that they are their own experts in this area, and that you are there simply to ask some questions. Use the group's wisdom to deflect any belief that you are the expert in this area. As always, avoid preaching or teaching, especially during this activity.

3. *Some men may not see any connection between their childhood family environment and their violent behaviors.* Discuss the program principle that behaviors are learned and may be passed on from generation to generation. Give them the opportunity to disagree and encourage their participation as much as possible.

4. *Some men may have difficulty drawing a family tree because of the complexity and changes in their family of origin.* Tell them to focus on the people with whom they were most involved while growing up. Suggest that they include people who aren't in the bloodline but were considered part of the family, such as close friends of the family.

5. *In discussing discipline, the topic of spanking usually arises.* Some men will argue that spanking is necessary to control children and that today's children aren't spanked or punished enough. Let them express their views. Some men rationalize spanking their children by explaining that they were spanked as children, too. They may say, "I deserved what I got" or "Getting whipped helped make me a better person." A positive response to the latter is "I believe you didn't deserve any of that and you turned out to be an okay person in spite of being whipped, not because of it."

At some point during the discussion, make clear your belief that spanking is not acceptable. The goal is to learn creative, nonabusive forms of discipline.

6. *Some men may have experienced abuse or violence within the school setting.* Discuss those experiences, including anyone who may have been abusive to them while they were going through school. Discuss their general impression of school and whether they "fit in" with other

kids. Some men may focus mainly on their older teenage years; while these years are important, help them to try to identify times when they were in elementary school, when they were much more vulnerable. Recalling this vulnerability may be helpful in building empathy later on.

7. *Help the men talk about what violence they observed within school, outside of school, and in the media.* Discuss what it felt like to see violence. Help them connect what they observed with their behavior later in life. Ask them if they made any promises to themselves about ways they would never act as adults, and then later found themselves acting in those ways.

8. *Emphasize the fact that their family of origin experiences did not cause them to act abusively toward their partner.* Identifying that these experiences may have influenced their decision to be abusive can help them take increased responsibility for their behavior. Sometimes men try to minimize their abusive behavior by blaming it on their experiences as a child. Point out that as horrible as their past may have been, they still had choices about how they would *act* toward others.

9. *Help them discuss, at length, the decisions they made about how they should act as boys and as men, particularly on dates and with girls.* Find out when they made those decisions, and what factors contributed to them. Connect this with how they want their children to grow up. What kinds of messages do they want to send their children about how men and women should relate to one another?

10. *This activity may bring up your own family of origin issues.* Be aware of your personal boundaries as well as what information about yourself you are willing to share. Seek professional support when needed.

Notes, comments, and observations:

Goals

In this activity, you will:

1. Better understand how your family of origin affects your behavior, particularly abusive behavior.

2. Understand that even though your family of origin may have influenced your decision to be violent, you are still responsible for your violent actions.

3. Understand the messages you received as a child that modeled abusive ways of solving problems.

4. Better understand those experiences that affected your feelings, thoughts, and behaviors while growing up.

5. Become more aware of the attitudes you were exposed to as a child that carry over into adulthood, particularly attitudes about women.

WORKSHEET 18   Family Tree

Draw a family tree showing who was in your family and how you were related. Include divorces, deaths, stepparents, stepbrothers, and stepsisters. Include as many relatives as you can remember, and reach as far back as you can remember. Also include any friends of the family who were especially close or influential.

WORSHEET 19	Family of Origin

WORKSHEET 19   **Family of Origin**

1. Who did you grow up with?

2. What is your overall feeling about growing up in your family—happy, fearful, sad, angry? What experiences contributed to these feelings?

3. What do you remember about how your mother was treated by her partner (your father, stepfather, or mother's partner)?

4. Who had the most power in your family when you were growing up? How did you know this person had the most power?

5. Some of the rules around the house were:

6. Who usually punished you when you were growing up?

7. When you were disciplined as a child:

   a. What did your father do?

   b. When he did this, how did you feel?

   c. What did your mother do?

   d. When she did this, how did you feel?

8. How did your mother or father usually punish you? How did you feel when punished this way?

9. What is your overall feeling about your school experience? What experiences contributed to these feelings?

10. Growing up, when did you feel the most comfortable and safe? How old were you?

11. Who did you look up to most when you were growing up? Why did you look up to this person?

12. When growing up . . .

   a. I thought girls were:

   b. I thought boys could:

   c. when it came to sex, I thought boys should:

   d. when it came to sex, I thought girls should:

   e. I thought boys' friends should always be:

   f. I thought boys should always play with:

   g. I thought men should always:

   h. I thought women should always:

(continued)

13. Who taught you what it meant to be a man? What did you like about this person?

14. Name one thing you swore you would *never* do when you grew up:

15. How has this thought affected your behavior?

16. Who showed you it was okay to be violent? Who showed you how to use abuse as a way to solve problems?

17. What negative, unhealthy attitudes or behaviors have you learned from others?

18. What can you do to change these unhealthy learned behaviors and attitudes?

Alcohol and Other Drugs

Goals

Upon completing this activity participants will:

1. Understand that alcohol and other drug use does not cause domestic abuse but may be a factor in it.

2. Make a list of personal signals that tell them they may start drinking or using other drugs.

3. Understand the personal consequences of their alcohol or other drug use.

4. Develop a plan to remain free of alcohol and other drugs as part of their goal of refraining from domestic abuse.

Required Worksheets

Alcohol and Other Drugs (Worksheet 20)
Staying Free of Alcohol and Other Drugs (Worksheet 21)

Format

Discuss at length the issue of alcohol and other drugs and how they affect people. Take a poll within the group to find out how many men were drinking alcohol or using another drug when arguing with a partner. Ask them why they think the numbers are so high (or low, depending on the group). Explain that a great percentage of the men who enter the domestic abuse program—about six out of ten—have had some alcohol or other drug abuse involved with their violence. Thus, it is important for everyone to consider the effects of these substances. Point out that these substances can make it difficult to recognize one's escalation signals, especially during intense or anxious situations. In many ways, the use of alcohol or other drugs may heighten the probability of violent behavior.

Ask the men to turn to Worksheet 20, Alcohol and Other Drugs. Give them fifteen minutes to fill out the worksheet, and explain that they will be talking about their responses with the rest of the group. When the group reassembles, let the men lead their own discussion of the first two questions. Have them ask for and discuss each other's responses.

When they have discussed the first two questions, write the headings from question three on the board. These headings are *Situations, Time of day, People you are with, Your feelings,* and *Your thoughts.* Ask the men for their responses to question three—signals that tell them they may use alcohol or other drugs—and record them in the appropriate column.

Prompt the discussion of triggers for alcohol and other drug use by asking about stresses in their life, such as their job, certain people, their home life, as well as normal situations where they might use chemicals, such as get-togethers with friends. Help them identify and examine their feelings and thoughts during these situations.

Next, lead them through a discussion of the remaining questions on the worksheet. Help them identify their behaviors when they use alcohol or other drugs. Ask them to list situations when they have been drinking and became abusive. Reinforce the principle that they are in control of themselves even when drinking or using other drugs.

Next, ask them to state the consequences and losses that result from their behavior. List these on the chalkboard. Encourage them to discuss the extent of the impact of their chemical use, and to rate those consequences from least meaningful (1) to most meaningful (10). In short, help them fully consider the negative impact of their alcohol and other drug use, particularly when they feel tense or anxious, or are in situations that require judgment and self-control.

Ask the men to turn to Worksheet 21, Staying Free of Alcohol and Other Drugs. Explain that they are to complete this plan with the intent of using it in their own life. Thus they must answer the questions with specific responses that fit for them. After they've had fifteen minutes to write their plan, reassemble the group and have each man talk about his plan for remaining free of alcohol and other drugs. Validate and affirm the positive steps or commitments they make as they state their process and describe their plan.

Issues

1. *Often men will say that their drug use or their drinking was the cause of their abusive behaviors.* Many times men will say that they were out of control and that they did not know what they were doing when they were drinking alcohol or using other drugs. Give them the opportunity to talk about feeling out of control in these situations. Discuss the issue of control and taking responsibility for one's own actions. Some men may refuse to admit that they were in control of their behaviors. With these men, you can ask why they did not inflict more serious harm on (or even kill) their partner if they were so out of control. This helps them understand that at some point they *did* have enough control to stop, no matter what drug they were using. For some men, it helps to direct their attention towards what they were feeling and thinking prior to using alcohol or other drugs. As you continue through this

activity, it will be obvious that they need to examine why they chose to use alcohol or other drugs and therefore, why they need to identify their signals so they can avoid becoming abusive.

2. *Some men say that alcohol or other drug use has never been a factor in their abusive behavior.* Discuss their point of view. Be sure that you reinforce your belief that alcohol and other drug use heightens the probability of abuse. Discuss their behaviors before they use alcohol or other drugs in comparison to their behaviors after they use. When men say that chemical use does not affect their behavior or thoughts at all, ask them to consider why driving while intoxicated laws have been developed and the reasons behind organizations such as Mothers Against Drunk Driving (MADD). Ask how many men would knowingly go out and drive while impaired by alcohol or other drugs, and how many would want their partners, children, parents, and friends to stay away from an impaired driver. Avoid power struggles and seek professional support to better deal with those men who are in denial of problem behaviors.

3. *Discuss the rule for the program regarding the use of alcohol and other drugs.* Talk about the program policy, the purpose behind it, and anything else that would be helpful for them to be aware of. Explain that because chemicals impair judgment, people under the influence tend to be less able to recognize quickly the signals of their escalating abusive behavior signals. Denial is often a major problem for people who think that they are not addicted or who are experiencing problems as a result of their substance use. If some group members continue to state that they do not have a problem, then frame your comments in terms of your hope that they will be able to maintain their control and to be responsible for their behaviors.

4. *Alcohol and other drugs impair the part of the brain responsible for judgment.* In this sense, use of alcohol and other drugs may make abuse more likely. At the same time, men who want to commit abuse may consciously choose to use chemicals because they intuitively understand that their behavior under the influence is more likely to be "forgiven." Or they may choose to use the chemicals to block the signals that they are going to become abusive, or to justify their violent behavior. Or they may use chemicals at an inappropriate time, leading to a relaxation of inhibitions and subsequent violence. Regardless of the reason, these men must therefore learn to identify the signals that they may be using alcohol or other drugs as part of their escalation.

5. *Be clear that violence and chemical dependency are two separate issues, both of which need attention.* Note that even if a man is involved in a recovery program for chemical dependency, domestic abuse may continue. Therefore, the man recovering from chemical dependency must still address his domestic abuse issues. Similarly, refraining from domestic abuse does not mean a person will be able to manage chemical dependency.

6. *Often men who are both abusive and chemically dependent have difficulty understanding the effects of their behaviors on other people.* Concentrate on the consequences of such men's behaviors, especially the negative impact on job, partner, and family. Discuss with these men (or the group as a whole) the issues of denial and minimizing in both chemical dependency and domestic abuse. Be blunt about the fact that there are plenty of chemically dependent people in the world who *do not* abuse their partners.

7. *Discussion of their signals is paramount.* The group members need to identify for themselves the signals that precede situations where they drink or use other drugs and may become violent. A man who avoids identifying such signals may be in denial of the consequences of chemical use in his life. Use the group to help the man confront his denial. Help them ask him some of the following questions:

   • What are the consequences of your chemical use?

   • Are those consequences severe enough to change your behavior?

   • Who is affected by your chemical use and ultimately, your violence?

   • Are there any alternatives to your chemical use and violence at this time?

8. *Help the group members develop their plans.* Their plans will help them avoid situations where they may use alcohol or other drugs and possibly become violent. Thus, they will stay safe and help others to stay safe, too. Help them understand that the plan is a way of taking care of themselves. (Note that no plan will totally help those who are chemically dependent quit using chemicals. A chemically dependent man may need ongoing treatment; at the very least, contact with such a man's court worker would be in order.)

9. *The support system is critical to staying free of alcohol and other drugs and to maintaining a violence-free life.* Some men resist this part of the plan by refusing to name specific people they can talk with or by refusing to commit to the plan. Part of the problem may be a fear of change; it is easier to stay the same. Help them recognize the importance of commitment to a specific plan, and of taking the risk to change.

Notes, comments, and observations:

Goals

In this activity, you will:

1. Understand that alcohol and other drug use does not cause domestic abuse but may play a part in it.

2. Make a list of personal signals that show you may start drinking or using other drugs.

3. Understand the personal consequences of your alcohol or other drug use.

4. Develop a plan to remain free of alcohol and other drugs as part of your goal of refraining from domestic abuse.

WORSHEET 20 — Alcohol and Other Drugs

WORKSHEET 20   **Alcohol and Other Drugs**

1. How often do you drink alcohol or use other drugs? What substances do you use?

2. List reasons why you use alcohol or other drugs:

3. What signals tell you that you may drink or use other drugs:

Situations	Time of day	People you are with	Your feelings	Your thoughts

4. How do you act when you drink or use other drugs?

5. What consequences result from your chemical use? What are your losses?

6. List and describe the situations in which you have been drinking or using other drugs and have become abusive:

7. Who has expressed concern about your use of alcohol or other drugs?

8. What do these concerns and consequences mean to you?

May Not Be Reproduced

WORKSHEET 21   Staying Free of Alcohol and Other Drugs

1. List your signals before using alcohol or other drugs:

2. List the messages you can give yourself about the possible consequences if you were to start using alcohol or other drugs:

3. List three alternatives to using alcohol or other drugs:

   a.

   b.

   c.

4. Name three people you can contact or talk with about alcohol and other drug use:

   a.

   b.

   c.

5. List other ways to stay sober or receive support for staying free of alcohol and other drugs:

May Not Be Reproduced

Goals

After completing this activity, participants will:

1. Increase their understanding of how abusive behavior affected their sexual relationship.

2. Increase their awareness of their attitudes about sexuality.

3. Better understand how attitudes about sexuality affect nonviolent problem solving.

4. Better understand their perspective on and values about sexuality.

Sex and Sexuality (Worksheet 22)

Required Worksheet Format

Discuss the term "sexuality" with the group. Brainstorm definitions and examples of sexuality and list these on the chalkboard. Talk about the differences of how men's and women's sexuality are portrayed in the media.

Ask the men to turn to the Sex and Sexuality Worksheet and fill it out as the discussion continues.

Write "male" and "female" in two columns at the top of the chalkboard. Ask the men to list words for male and female genitals and other sexual characteristics. Write the words down as the men speak. Discuss the difference between the two lists. Examine the primarily negative connotations of terms for the female anatomy. Ask how these connotations affect the men's view of male and female sexuality.

Discuss the sexual expectations of boys and girls in dates and relationships. Ask some of the following questions:

- Who was supposed to make the first move?

- What does the language of "getting to first base" and "going all the way" imply about the role of sex?

- How was the girl supposed to react when the boy made sexual advances?

- Was it okay for the girl to say "stop" at any point during the situation?

- Who was responsible for saying "no" to being sexual?

- Who was responsible for contraception?

- What did other guys say about their dates with girls?

- How did you learn all these rules?

Discuss the difference between exploring one's maleness and being sexual with a partner. The first has more to do with understanding who men are and how to be male, while being sexual implies a range of behaviors from language to intercourse. Talk about what it means to "be sexual," and help the men recognize the difference between exploring their maleness and being sexual. Point out that many men use being sexual as a way to prove their masculinity; thus sexuality (or masculinity) gets confused with sexual activity.

Ask the group to brainstorm ideas of how to meet their needs to feel masculine and how to meet their needs to be sexual. Make lists, on the chalkboard, of masculine needs and sexual needs. Discuss the differences in the lists. Explain that these are two separate issues that need to be explored. When these two issues get connected, they contribute to the view of women as objects, always able and willing to meet men's sexual needs. When a woman does not fulfill this perceived obligation, men view her as negative or a "bitch." This leads to a view of women as bad and men as good, or a view that men are more important than women.

Examine how being sexual with a partner affects the relationship. Ask questions such as, "Was it your goal to be sexual with this person?" "How did your relationship change after your sexual experience with that person—were there new expectations?" Explore how the men's past values, the messages they received about sex, and their current beliefs about sex in relationships have affected their behavior toward their partners.

Ask the men to list conflicts they have had with partners related to being sexual. Discuss what would happen if one or the other person wanted to be sexual and the other did not.

Brainstorm and list on the chalkboard ways that a sexual relationship is changed by abuse. Ask some of the following questions:

- How might your partner feel about being sexual with you after you have hit her or threatened her?

- What might she be thinking if she refuses?

- If she does refuse, how would you feel?

- What would you do if she refuses?

Discuss jealousy, and how a man's partner might feel if accused of having sex with someone else. Point out that a woman may genuinely love a man but still spend time talking and being friendly with other men.

To close the activity, discuss what has been helpful about examining sexuality, what they have learned about themselves, and one way they will take care of themselves in this area.

Issues

1. *Sex is difficult for some men to discuss.* Most men have been used to joking about sex or talking about it in ways that degrade women. Give them some time to feel more comfortable with the area as they discuss it. Understand that inappropriate comments, laughing, and avoidance are techniques they use to deal with their embarrassment. If needed, remind them of any program expectations related to respect of others. In general, there is a great deal of negative self-talk around the issue of sex. Thus, it's important to have the men talk about how they will change this negative self-talk, and it is important to model and practice this behavior in the group setting.

2. *Some men will minimize or deny having conflicts over being sexual with a partner as a problem.* It may be helpful to allow them to talk about other men or describe situations using a third person pronoun to escape any shame or embarrassment.

3. *Some men may try to use this time to brag about their male prowess.* Guide the discussion to focus on how abusive behavior can affect their sexual relationship with their partner. Discuss marital rape and their views of this issue. Avoid power struggles and encourage group members to state how their violent behaviors affected their sexual relationship.

4. *Emphasize the importance of their escalation signals surrounding their sexual needs and violent behavior.* Sexuality is often a red flag area for these men. Help them understand and stay aware of their escalation signals when they are in a situation in which their sexual needs differ from their partners. The men may have difficulty empathizing with their partners, but often they will be able to begin to identify the signals that could lead to abusive behaviors. Avoid trying to convince group members about how their partner may think. Focus on ways they can avoid being abusive when they are wanting their sexual needs to be met. Some role-plays may be helpful at this time.

5. *Jealousy and affairs are common themes that surface during this activity.* Jealousy is stated in terms of needing to watch their partner, or make sure she is not doing something he does not want her to do. Identify jealousy as a feeling and not necessarily a bad thing. Explain

that jealousy becomes destructive when the men jump to conclusions as a result of the feeling, and then act on those erroneous conclusions. Help the men understand that feelings of jealousy are related to spoken and unspoken expectations in the relationship. Focus on the men's expectations and how they will take care of themselves if their partner makes choices they do not like. Some men may use the excuse that "if she doesn't have sex with me, then I'll find someone else to have sex with." Examine the effects of this attitude and behavior on the relationship. Point out that it can result in attempts to control and manipulate their partner and their sexual relationship.

A related statement often made is, "Well, she keeps saying I'm making love with someone else, so I may as well do it." This statement may confirm a dissatisfaction in the current relationship. Help the man understand that he needs to examine his intentions and goals in the relationship.

◆◆◆

Notes, comments, and observations:

Participant's Workbook Sample

Goals

In this activity, you will:

1. Increase your understanding of how abusive behavior affected your sexual relationship.

2. Increase your awareness of your attitudes about sexuality.

3. Better understand how attitudes about sexuality affect nonviolent problem solving.

4. Better understand your perspective on and values about sexuality.

Worksheet 22   Sex and Sexuality

1. How have women been treated as sex objects in the media and by society? (Give examples.)

2. Words and phrases that are used to describe men and men's genitals:

3. Words and phrases that are used to describe women and women's genitals:

4. What are the differences between the two lists?

5. With regards to sex how were boys supposed to act on a date?

6. With regards to sex how were girls supposed to act on a date?

7. What conflicts have you had with partners about being sexual?

8. If you wanted to be sexual and your partner didn't, what would you do?

9. What would she do?

10. If she wanted to be sexual and you didn't, what would you do?

11. What would she do?

12. How have your abusive behaviors affected your sexual relationship with your partner?

13. What are the signals that your abusive behavior is affecting your sexual relationship?

14. Using the assertive approach, develop nonabusive ways to handle the following situations:

    a. You are watching TV, about ready to go to bed, and feel like being sexual with your partner. You ask her about it, and she begins to argue with you. She says, "You always want sex whenever you want it, and never consider me."

    b. It has been three months since you and your partner have been sexual together. You say, "Let's have some fun tonight." She says she can't forget about the last time you got violent with her, so she doesn't want to "have fun tonight."

May Not Be Reproduced

Cluster 3

Becoming Accountable

Letters to the People I Have Abused

Goals

In this activity, participants will:

1. Better understand how their abusive behaviors have affected others.

2. Take increased responsibility for their abusive behaviors.

3. Gain insight into why they have been abusive.

Required Worksheet

Letters to the People I Have Abused (Worksheet 23)

Format

Review with the men the importance of accepting responsibility for abusive behavior. Discuss how writing letters is a specific way of taking increased responsibility for their abusive behaviors. Explain that they will be writing two letters, but that neither letter will be sent at this time. Ask the men to turn to the worksheet, Letters to the People I Have Abused. Read the first paragraph and give the group five minutes to list the first names of the people they have abused. Then ask them to select two of these people to write to. You can choose to give them time to write the letters during the group session, or send the worksheets home with them as work to be done for a follow-up session. Explain that they should answer the next six questions on the worksheet within their letters. Encourage them to use a letter format or style rather than listing their answers to the questions.

During a follow-up session or after they have written their letters, have the men read their letters to the group. After each person reads, ask the others to use the questions on the worksheet to clarify the man's letter. After all the group members have shared, ask them to complete the final two questions. Give them five minutes to write their answers. Discuss in group their answers to these questions. Ask some of the following questions:

- What did you learn from this exercise?

- What was the most difficult part of writing the letters?

- What did it feel like to hear other member's letters?

- How did you benefit from this exercise?

Finish the group session by having each man share a characteristic strength or something he likes about himself. Provide support and give them credit for completing this activity.

1. *Discussion of the process, goals, and purpose of this activity is essential.* Clarification will help the men accept this activity as something that may benefit them. They may fear that the wrong person might see their letters. Assure them that *they* will decide who sees the letters. They will not be required to mail the letters.

2. *Some men may be unable or unwilling to make a list of the first names of people they have abused.* Discuss this in the group. If a man is unable to think of anyone to write to, ask other group members for suggestions. Sometimes it helps to let a reluctant man know he won't have to read his letter first. If everyone has shared and he still refuses, discuss the group rules and program policy regarding participation in the group. Seek professional and collegial support for ways to work with this man in group.

3. *Make special arrangements for men who are unable to read or write.* Allow for some flexibility with *all* the men by suggesting alternatives to this activity, such as audio recording, dictating a letter to you, a friend, or another group member, or drawing a picture of the story. For an individual with special needs, present these options before the group session begins.

4. *Let them use any style of writing they wish.* The idea here is that they personalize the activity so that it does not get minimized. Have them write the letters *to* a specific person, not *about* the person, using "I" and "me." This helps them take personal responsibility for their actions. Have them write a greeting, the body of the letter, and a closing remark before their name, so that they think of this as a real letter and not an exercise.

5. *During and after the time a man reads his letter, ask yourself, other group members, and the man some of the following questions:*

   - Has he answered the guideline questions from the worksheet?

   - Is he minimizing his behaviors?

   - Is he blaming the other person for his behaviors?

   - Should he rewrite the letter?

   - What were the strengths of the letter?

6. *When the group is giving input to a letter, encourage them to think about some of the above questions.* Guide the group's comments to balance their challenging and supportive statements.

7. *This can be a very powerful activity.* Encourage the men to talk at length about how it felt to do this exercise. Discuss what they have learned as well as what you have learned about each of them. After reading the letters they may feel vulnerable and ashamed (although

they may show these feelings in a variety of ways). Talk about these feelings and ask them if they need to know anything further from you or other group members. Help them understand that there is a difference between their humanity and their decisions to act abusively. Expect them to be angry with you for having them do this activity; these men often react with anger when they feel vulnerable. The exercise can also build positive group cohesion. Recognize this dynamic and emphasize the need to support and challenge each other outside of the group setting.

Notes, comments, and observations:

Goals

In this activity, you will:

1. Better understand how your abusive behaviors have affected others.

2. Take increased responsibility for your abusive behaviors.

3. Gain insight into why you have been abusive.

WORSHEET 23 Letters to the People I Have Abused

There are two reasons to write letters to the people you have abused. One is to gain more insight into your behavior. The other is to begin to take more responsibility for your actions. You don't have to mail these letters.

List all the people you have directly or indirectly abused in any way or form:

- _____
- _____
- _____
- _____
- _____

- _____
- _____
- _____
- _____
- _____

Circle the names of those people you will write a letter to (at least two).

Here are some questions to think about when you write this letter:
- What abuse did you do?
- How do you feel about what you did?
- How did you feel when you were escalating in these situations?
- How are your partner and kids affected by your abusive actions? (How might she feel, what might she think you will do to her in the future, what did she have to stop or change in order for you to get your way, how did her life have to change?)
- What are you doing to take responsibility for your abusive actions?
- What do you want from these people now?

After you have written the letters, answer the following questions:
- If you send these letters, how might the other people be affected?
- How would you feel if you sent these letters?

May Not Be Reproduced

Personal Accountability Plan

Goals

In this activity, participants will:

1. Better understand how to be accountable for their abusive behaviors.

2. Take responsibility for their abusive behaviors.

3. Develop a plan to be responsible and accountable for their abusive behaviors.

Required Worksheet

Personal Accountability Plan (Worksheet 24)

Format

Discuss the terms "accountability" and "responsibility" and their similarities. In the dictionary they are considered synonymous. Provide the definition (trustworthy; able to answer for one's conduct and obligations) and then ask the group for their definitions. Record their responses on the chalkboard. Discuss the meaning of accountability using the terms given by group members.

Explain how in a business, workers are accountable to supervisors, who are accountable to managers, who are accountable to the executives, who are accountable to the chief executive, who is accountable to the Board of Directors, who are accountable to the consumers of the product made by the business.

Ask the men to whom they are accountable at home, at work, and in society. Then examine to whom *those* people are accountable until there are three or four levels of accountability and the lines of interrelatedness are crossing and connecting with many other people. Chart these layers of accountability on the chalkboard. The main point to emphasize is that everyone is accountable to someone.

Examine to whom they are accountable for their abusive behaviors. Chart these layers of accountability on the chalkboard. Again, develop up to four levels of accountability with interconnecting lines.

Ask the men to open their workbooks to the Personal Accountability Plan Worksheet. Give the men ten minutes to record the information from the board onto their workbooks onto Diagram 1, but instruct them to develop the accountability charts using names of people and levels of accountability that are true for them. Briefly discuss their responses, then have them complete Diagram 2 and discuss that.

Prior to this activity, create a list of suggestions for being accountable. Some of these might include:

- Volunteer time to work with child victims or witnesses of abuse.

- Volunteer time at a battered women's shelter.

- Colead a men's domestic abuse group.

- Talk about your history to a reporter.

- Make presentations to police, judges, clergy, and so forth about your experience with domestic abuse.

- Talk to groups of men about your journey.

- Address and challenge other men's abusive behavior.

- Attend a continuing care support group.

- Speak to groups of adolescents about your abusive behaviors and ways you take care of yourself now.

Distribute the list to the men. Explain that these are some ways some other men have remained accountable for their behaviors. Ask them to turn back to the worksheet, Personal Accountability Plan, and give them time to fill in the chart labeled "Personal Accountability Plan," using people from their Accountability Diagram 2. When they have completed their plan ask some of the following questions:

- What prevents you from being accountable to others? (For example, self-talk.)

- What are some positive alternatives to think about to get past the above obstacles?

- How does it feel to be accountable to others?

- What might you gain from being accountable for your abusive behaviors?

When the group is ready, have each member select and talk about two of the people they will be accountable to and what they will do to demonstrate their accountability. Insist that they specify when they will have completed the commitment. Have them write these commitments onto their worksheets. If they want to change any part of this commitment, they need to explain the change to the group first.

Explain that at a follow-up session (a date specified by you), they will report on their progress with their accountability plans. During the follow-up session, have each member talk about his commitments and update or change them if necessary. Follow-ups should be done periodically throughout the final weeks of the program. During one of the last group sessions, their accountability plans should be updated and changed to reflect their plans once the program has ended.

Issues

1. *Accountability is the action part of responsibility.* When someone demonstrates that they are being responsible, they are being accountable. This may be a difficult concept for the men to grasp. You can explain it in terms of putting words into action: not just "talking the talk," but also "walking the walk."

2. *Many men may resist moving beyond admission of abuse to developing an accountability plan.* Affirm them for acknowledging their abusive behavior. Ask how they will maintain an abuse-free frame of mind. Explore and examine their plans for not acting violently or abusively in the future. Use these ideas to develop part of their accountability plan. Then work backward to the names of people they will be accountable to.

   Some men may not like the term "accountability." Help them get familiar and comfortable with it. Some of the discomfort may be related to understanding its meaning.

3. *Accountability can be demonstrated in many ways and on many levels.* There is no definitive way for every man in the group. Encourage each man to individualize his plan. As each man discusses his accountability plan, consider:

   - Is the plan realistic?

   - Can he do it by himself (so he won't blame others if he fails to keep his commitment)?

   - Is he trying to do too much at once?

   - Is he comfortable with his plan?

   - How much will his plan challenge him and enhance his growth?

4. *Remember, some men may say they are not ready to be accountable at this time in their life.* They may refuse to be accountable beyond stating they have been abusive, or believe that they have been accountable by going to jail or participating in the abuse group. Direct their attention to abuse as a lifelong problem that needs ongoing attention. Explain that this exercise is an opportunity to plan for this ongoing attention rather than forgetting it all after a few months or until their next act of abuse and resulting negative consequences.

5. *Some men may feel overwhelmed by the number of people they are accountable to for their abusive behaviors.* Discuss these feelings. Ask them (or yourself) some of the following questions:

- What makes accountability overwhelming for these men?

- What are the feelings underneath the sense of being overwhelmed?

- Do they feel different about being accountable to one person versus another?

- Why is it easier to be responsible (talk) than to be accountable (act)?

- How do they minimize or deny the obligation to be accountable?

- What gains can be made by being accountable? How can they benefit?

6. *As each member discusses his accountability plans, guide the men to develop even more options for their own plans.* Suggest that they brainstorm more options, and not be satisfied with only one or two options.

7. *Some of the men may get stuck or be unable to develop a plan.* If necessary, demonstrate the process with a couple of volunteers to model what the plans could look like. Then give the men ten minutes to complete their own plans.

8. *Remind the group that this activity does not fix, cure, or justify their behaviors in the future.* These plans become concrete reminders to act nonviolently in future situations. This is an ongoing process. Sometimes they may make mistakes, but they have begun to build a foundation to counteract years of pro-violence messages from society. No one can take this foundation from them, and what they build upon it cannot be destroyed. Their willingness to change by being accountable for the poor decisions they made in the past is really an example of taking care of themselves.

Notes, comments, and observations:

Participant's Workbook Sample

Goals

In this activity, you will:

1. Better understand how to be accountable for your abusive behaviors.

2. Take responsibility for your abusive behaviors.

3. Develop a plan to be responsible and accountable for your abusive behaviors.

WORKSHEET 24	Personal Accountability Plan

1. What is accountability?

2. Accountability Diagram 1
   (Who are you accountable to at work, at home, in society, on the street?)

YOU

3. Accountability Diagram 2
   (Who are you accountable to for your abusive behaviors?)

YOU

4. How does it feel to be accountable to people?

5. How can you benefit from being accountable for your abusive behaviors?

(continued)

6. Personal Accountability Plan

Who are you accountable to for your abusive behavior?	What do you need to do to be accountable?	What do you gain from being accountable to this person?	How will you get support to help you remain accountable to this person?

7. To be accountable, you need to commit to specific actions with specific people. Select two people from the list you just made and describe exactly what you will do to become accountable.

   1. a. *Who* you will be accountable to:
       b. Describe exactly *what* you will do to show that you are accountable:
       c. Exactly *when* you will have accomplished this:

   2. a. *Who* you will be accountable to:
       b. Describe exactly *what* you will do to show that you are accountable:
       c. Exactly *when* you will have accomplished this:

Cluster 4

Tools for Nonviolence

Self-Talk

Goals

In this activity, participants will:

1. Better understand the influence of self-talk on their behavior.

2. Increase their positive self-talk.

3. Develop a positive self-talk plan.

Required Worksheets

Self-Talk List (Worksheet 25)
Self-Talk Plan (Worksheet 26)
Self-Talk Record (Worksheet 27)

Format

Examine and discuss situations when the men feel angry, happy, content, nervous, anxious, or tense. Introduce the concept of self-talk and discuss what self-talk means to each group member. Ask the men to identify messages that they say to themselves in all sorts of situations. Write their responses on the chalkboard. Read the following statements and discuss the self-talk they use when they hear them.

- You're doing a good job.

- I don't like what you just did.

- I hate you!

- Moron!

- You hurt me.

- You are not a father to my children.

- Lazy slob!

- Get a job.

- I like your clothes.

- That woman over there is pretty good-looking.

Discuss the differences when these statements are made by a partner, fellow employee, stranger, or family member. Explain how self-talk can determine how you feel for short periods and long periods of time. Ask group members to give examples of how they have already used self-talk to get out of a depressed mood or to get down on themselves by calling themselves names. Examine messages that they give themselves when they are starting to escalate, feel upset, or get angry.

Ask the men to turn to Worksheet 25, the Self-Talk List. Explain that they will have ten minutes to complete the worksheet. When they are finished, discuss their responses and list them on the chalkboard. After everyone has talked about the messages they say to themselves as they escalate, make another column on the chalkboard and brainstorm alternative messages. List these messages on the chalkboard, and ask the men to fill those in on their worksheet.

Explain that just as a responsibility plan helps them prepare options for responsible behavior in tense moments, a self-talk plan can prepare them with positive messages to use during stressful and difficult times. Have the group turn to Worksheet 26, their Self-Talk Plan. Ask them to list, in the far left column, typical tough situations they face. In the next column, they should list all the feelings they might have when those situations occur. For each feeling, ask them to write a positive self-talk message to deal with the situation and the feeling. Finally, have each man read aloud a feeling, the corresponding situation, and the self-talk message he plans on using to deal with the experience.

Emphasize that for each feeling, they need to have as many self-talk messages as possible, and that they should choose the ones that fit for them. Discuss the difference between helpful and hurtful self-talk for the specific feelings. When they have all reported their plans, ask them to fill in at least three ways they will remember to use these new messages (for example, they may write them down, put them up on the refrigerator, and so forth). This plan is meant to help the men take a proactive step toward integrating positive alternatives into their behaviors.

Ask them to turn to Worksheet 27, Self-Talk Record. Explain that they are to monitor and record their self-talk, feelings, and behaviors during the next week. They will be asked to share some of these experiences with the rest of the group.

Follow-Up

During the follow-up session, have each group member discuss a self-talk message they had in the past week. After all the group members have talked, ask some of the following questions:

- What have you learned from this activity?

- How can you plan to give yourself positive self-talk?

- Who can you talk to or where can you go to get support for maintaining a positive self-talk plan?

- What do you need from others to help this plan succeed?

Issues

1. *Some group members may have difficulty understanding the concept of self-talk.* Try to make your explanations as concrete as possible. Ask them what they are thinking at the moment you are speaking. Explain that these thoughts are what they are telling themselves—self-talk.

2. *Emphasize the connection between what they tell themselves and how they feel.* Give many examples and have group members talk from their own experience. Explain that when they pay attention to their self-talk and learn to control it, they can influence how they feel and the intensity of that feeling. Changing their self-talk takes a great deal of practice and motivation. Discuss how someone can "self-talk" themselves into a rage, but with some practice and awareness, can reverse or alter the thinking to get to a feeling that is more manageable.

3. *It may be useful to help group members practice by acting out a self-talk situation.* Ask the group to come up with a situation which involves self-talk. Discuss what self-talk might be happening. Role-play the situation and have the person doing the self-talk describe the self-talk and the feelings associated with the situation. Discuss alternative messages to this self-talk and write these suggestions on the chalkboard. Role-play the situation again, only this time have the person verbalize the alternative self-talk messages. Discuss how it feels to use new self-talk. Do they feel uncomfortable? Do they feel a greater sense of self-control?

4. *Encourage group members to view self-talk as a signal.* Self-talk awareness can be a useful tool to deal with feelings and to take care of oneself. Explain that as they learn to pay attention to their self-talk, they will be better able to predict how they might react to a given situation.

5. *Many self-talk messages are derived from past events, and it is important for the men to identify and examine these messages and events.* Some men react violently or abusively when they feel belittled or feel a threat to their masculinity. It is important to help group members understand that they risk a great deal when they do identify and use positive self-talk.

6. *Reinforce the rewards and consequences of self-talk.* It takes work to change lifelong patterns. Men are more motivated when they understand exactly how they will benefit from the changes they make.

Notes, comments, and observations:

Participant's Workbook Sample

Goals

In this activity, you will:

1. Better understand the influence of self-talk on your behavior.

2. Increase your positive self-talk.

3. Develop a positive self-talk plan.

WORKSHEET 25   Self-Talk List

1. Check the messages you have said to yourself as you escalated. Add your own to the list:

   ☐ She's out to hurt me.   ☐ I don't give a rip.

   ☐ She doesn't love men.   ☐ She deserves it.

   ☐ She doesn't care about anything.   ☐ It's my house.

   ☐ She's always ragging on me.   ☐ I wish she'd shut up.

   ☐ I'm not angry.   ☐ I can handle my liquor (pot, crack).

   ☐ She's having sex with someone else.   ☐ I'm losing control of her.

   ☐ _____   ☐ _____

   ☐ _____   ☐ _____

2. List the messages you can use to avoid being abusive (see the self-talk list above) in difficult situations.

   a.

   b.

   c.

   d.

May Not Be Reproduced

WORSHEET 26 — Self-Talk Plan

You can plan ahead to use positive self-talk. Think of tough situations that often happen to you. List those in the first column. Next, think of all the feelings you might have in each situation (anger, fear, jealousy, and so forth). List these feelings in the middle column. In the final column, write a positive self-talk message to correspond with each feeling.

Situations	Possible feelings	Specific positive self-talk (one for each feeling)

Ways you can remember these self-talk statements:

a.

b.

c.

d.

e.

WORKSHEET 27 — Self-Talk Record

During the week of _____, record some of the messages you tell yourself:

Date	Message you told yourself	How you felt	What you did	Other messages you could tell yourself

Assertiveness

Goals

In this session, participants will:

1. Understand what assertiveness means.

2. Understand how assertive behavior is a way of taking responsibility for their actions.

3. Increase their assertiveness skills.

4. Develop an assertiveness plan suitable for many situations.

5. Develop a support system to nurture assertiveness skills.

Required Worksheets

Ways to Be Assertive (Worksheet 28)
Assertive Actions (Worksheet 29)
How Can You Be Assertive in These Situations? (Worksheet 30)
Assertive Behavior Record (Worksheet 31)
Assertiveness Strategy Plan (Worksheet 32)

Format

Write the following terms across the top of the chalkboard: passive, aggressive, and passive-aggressive. Begin with the passive column and ask the group members to give examples, definitions, or words and phrases that apply to this word. Ask some of the following questions:

- How does a person who behaves this way get what he wants?

- Does this person *always* get what he wants when he acts this way?

- Who gains or loses if a person acts this way? How?

- Can anyone *always* act this way?

- Can you identify one or two examples of how you have acted this way?

- How does it feel when you act this way?

- What are the rewards or consequences of acting this way?

- What is the goal of this action?

Record all their responses. Repeat this process (and these questions) with the remaining terms.

Following are some of the responses you'll probably hear:

Passive	Aggressive	Passive-Aggressive
weak	strong	anger
nerdy	abusive	indirect with feelings
stepped on	demanding	stepped on
quiet	loud	revengeful
someone has to guess how you feel	take what you want	don't always get what you want
other people have to give you what you want	hurtful	don't say real feeling, then be abusive
	intimidating	
indirect	hurt others	goal is to have others give you what you want, and when you don't get it, you punish the person
isolated	get what you want at all costs	
lonely	indirect with feelings	
doormat	angry	
don't always get what you want	goal is to take what you want	
goal is to get others to give you what you want		

When you have discussed all of the terms, erase everything on the chalkboard. Write "assertiveness" at the top of the board. Ask the group members to review the meaning of this action term, its rewards and consequences, how it feels to act assertively, and who gains or loses by acting assertively. Explain that in assertiveness, the goal is to say how you feel and what you want, and that asking questions places the other person on the defensive. Explore the risks in acting assertively, using "I" statements, and avoiding asking questions of the other party.

Here are some of the responses you can expect for the definition of assertiveness:

The assertive person

- Communicates clearly

- Is direct with feelings and wants

- May not always get what he wants

- Asks directly for what he wants

- Is responsible for the effort, not the outcome

- Uses "I" statements

- Has the goal of stating how he feels and what he wants (even though he might not get it)

Explain that no one is assertive all the time; being assertive takes more effort than being passive, aggressive, or passive-aggressive, especially since most of us have not learned to be assertive while growing up. Society reinforces nonassertive strategies more than assertive ones.

Stress the simplest of meanings for assertiveness by writing the definition:

To say how you feel or what you want.

Discuss some example situations that the group members suggest, including how they can say what they feel and what they want. Then write the following model statement on the board for them:

When I feel _____ I need to _____
and I want _____ .

Ask the men to turn to Worksheet 28, Ways to Be Assertive. Discuss these options and techniques. Explain and emphasize the effort it takes to use them. If possible have some of the men develop additional examples.

From this point in the activity there are several options you may choose to further practice the art of assertiveness. Practice and role-plays will occupy a great deal of time, and you can use Worksheet 30, How Can You Be Assertive in These Situations?, for extra practice scenarios. Also, it is helpful to choose some activities that break the group into smaller units, although to save time you can conduct any of these options by having a few volunteers act in front of the entire group.

Regardless of which option you choose, ask the men to turn to Worksheet 29, Assertive Actions.

Option One   Divide the men into groups of three. Explain that you will be giving the small groups several scenarios in which they can practice assertiveness skills. One person will play the partner and the other will play himself. The third man must record what the man playing himself does or says that is assertive. State that everyone will get the opportunity to play themselves, a partner, and a recorder.

At the end of the Format for this activity is a list of assertiveness role-plays (page 149). Read one of these scenarios to all three groups. Explain that the man playing himself has five minutes to make as many assertive statements or assertive actions as he possibly can. The man playing the partner can act it out any way he wishes, while the third man records the assertive statements and actions.

After they complete the first five minutes, have them switch roles. Read a new scenario and repeat the process. Finally, choose another scenario and repeat the process a third time.

Ask for two volunteers to act out the scenario and one man to keep time. Read one of the role-plays and have the two men act out the situation, encouraging one to act assertively and to make as many assertive statements as possible within three minutes. Have the rest of the group help the man out by suggesting assertive statements. Repeat this process with other volunteers as long as time permits.
Option Two

Combine Options One and Two. Have the men practice in smaller groups, but ask only one or two groups to perform a role-play for the large group.
Option Three

Regardless of the option you choose, after everyone has practiced, bring the group together to discuss the scenarios and the ways men were assertive. List the options men used under the heading "assertiveness" on the chalkboard.

Discuss the amount of effort and energy it takes to be assertive. Review how it feels to be assertive and that the goal is simply to state how you feel and what you want. Explain that their natural tendency is to try to convince their partner to change her position or do something their way. But this tendency contradicts the goals of assertiveness and can easily lead them back into abusive behavior.

Discuss obstacles to acting assertively. Explain that most of the obstacles are self-talk messages that they've come to believe are true or that someone else gave them. Have them record some of their self-talk on their worksheets under the question, "What kinds of messages do you give yourself (self-talk) that stop you from being assertive?"

Next, help them develop a list of positive self-talk to overcome these obstacles to assertiveness. Emphasize that whether they act passively, aggressively, or assertively, they *have* made a choice about how to act. Have them write these messages on the worksheet in response to the question, "What kinds of self-talk can you use to be more assertive?"

Ask the men to write or describe two situations in which they and their partner had a disagreement. Tell them to list three ways of acting assertively in each of the situations; they can draw from the list of examples on the chalkboard, what others have talked about, and their own experience. Give the group ten minutes to complete the task.

Next, have each man pick one of the two situations and describe his three options. Encourage other group members to comment on and add to the man's options. Remind the group members that there are always a number of assertive options in any situation.

Discuss this entire activity and the way the men have begun to practice assertiveness. Ask some of the following:

• What part of this exercise was the most difficult?

• What part was the easiest?

• What have you learned?

• What was the most helpful to you during this exercise?

• What areas do you need more practice on?

• Where and from whom can you get support to act assertively?

Ask the men to turn to Worksheet 31, Assertive Behavior Record. Review the monitoring sheet with them. For the next week (or some other negotiated period of time) have the men monitor and record their assertive behaviors. Explain that the more they practice, the more natural assertiveness will be for them. Remind them that they can make a choice to be assertive in a stressful situation, and only they can control whether they act assertively or in some less healthy way. Let the group know that they will report on their progress at the next agreed-upon session.

Use Worksheet 32, Assertiveness Strategy Plan, as needed to provide additional assistance. This worksheet helps the men plan assertive responses to typical situations they encounter in their lives. Have the men take ten minutes to complete the chart. Discuss some of the other assertive tips on the worksheet, such as body language, and the formula for communicating assertively. Discuss one of the situations they described on their chart.

Follow-Up

At the follow-up session, ask each man to state how many times he felt he was assertive during the monitoring period. Ask him to pick one situation and describe it by answering all the questions on Worksheet 31, Assertive Behavior Record. Ask the other men for their observations. Repeat the process until all the group members have reported on their assertive behaviors.

One way to end each session on assertiveness is to have each man state one way that he will act assertively in the next week.

Assertiveness role-plays for use in this activity:

Scenario One
Your partner begins to yell at you about always coming home late and spending too much time with your friends.

Scenario Two
Your boss calls you into the office and says that you need to do better at your job. Your boss says other employees have stated that you are lazy and don't get your work done.

Scenario Three
Your sixteen-year-old son talks back to you regularly. You just got a call from school saying that he did not attend today.

Scenario Four
You just received four phone calls in which the person hung up as soon as you picked up the phone. Your partner takes a call a few minutes later, then tells you she has to go meet a friend for a few hours.

Scenario Five
Your partner starts telling you how angry she is about something you did to her four months ago. She begins to raise her voice.

Issues

1. *Assertiveness is often a new concept to men.* Men will confuse assertive actions with what they may think of as socially acceptable ways of being aggressive. Because most men are socialized to be aggressive, they often view nonaggressive behavior as effeminate; when they attempt to replace aggressive behavior, they choose passive or passive-aggressive behavior. That is why it is important for you to model assertiveness and help them understand the differences between assertiveness and the other action terms. Give the group plenty of time to discuss and get familiar with this new term. Remember that because this may be a foreign way of thinking and acting, it will take a lot of effort and time for them to adopt this new behavior.

2. *Let the group wrestle with the terms you are asking them to define.* Avoid just stating the "correct" answers and definitions in the beginning. Ask what they think of a man who acts this way—is he weak, strong, masculine, feminine, and so forth? Challenge their definitions. Often they will develop their own definitions that are superior to any of the standard psychological jargon—definitions which are believable and have practical application to their situations.

3. *Continually remind them that there are many assertive options in any given situation.* Many men look for an ultimate answer (especially from you) for how to be assertive. Avoid this by emphasizing the variety of choices found on Worksheet 28, Ways to Be Assertive. Also, remind the men that these are just examples and that there are countless other possibilities.

4. *Some men may refuse to participate in the role-plays.* Assure them that their acting ability is not being graded. The idea is to get some practice in using these tools. Depending on the option you choose, you may suggest that they will only be required to do this in small groups. Avoid power struggles over this issue; let this be a fun exercise. Allow the small groups to decide who goes first in what role, which may offer some safety for those who are reluctant players.

5. *As the men discuss their assertive actions, relate and compare their choices to the examples you've discussed earlier.* If a man believes his actions have been assertive when they've really been passive or aggressive, correct his belief or let the other group members point this out to him.

6. *Stress that their behaviors are a result of decisions they make about how to react.* In other words, they will choose to be assertive, aggressive, or passive. They are responsible for these choices and will receive rewards or consequences for their actions. The healthiest choice is to be assertive.

7. *Help them see that the goal of each of these actions is to get what they want.* If they are passive, someone else has to give them what they want. If they are aggressive, they take what they want. If they are assertive, they ask for what they want. See the chart below.

Passive	*Aggressive*	*Assertive*
A. I'm given what I want.	I take what I want.	I ask for what I want.
B. I get stepped on.	I step on others.	Both partners' needs are mutually maintained in an atmosphere of safety and with a desire to negotiate or come to a consensus.
C. I may or may not get what I want.	I may or may not get what I want.	I may or may not get what I want.

The common theme to all three action terms is C, "I may or may not get what I want." In every case, the risk exists of not getting your needs met. The other option—getting what you want through violence or other force—is simply not acceptable. So, the safest way of acting is to be assertive: ask for what you want and say how you feel.

8. *Going beyond "asking for what you want and saying how you feel" crosses the line from assertiveness to aggressiveness.* The goal is to be assertive and feel good about having been assertive. Trying to convince or force the other person to think, feel, or do what you want is an aggressive act.

9. *Teach them to concentrate on the key phrase, "I am responsible for the effort, not the outcome."* This positive self-talk helps men get beyond the obstacles to assertiveness. Encourage discussion of this phrase and its practical applications.

◆◆◆

Notes, comments, and observations:

Participant's Workbook Sample

Goals

In this session, you will:

1. Understand what assertiveness means.

2. Understand how assertive behavior is a way of taking responsibility for your actions.

3. Increase your assertiveness skills.

4. Develop an assertiveness plan you can use for many situations.

5. Develop a support system to nurture your assertiveness skills.

WORSHEET 28	**Ways to Be Assertive**

Here are some examples of how some men have chosen to be assertive:

"When you yell at me like that I feel like I'm being treated like a little kid. I am embarrassed and feel stupid. When I feel this way I need to let you know how I feel. I want to be treated like an adult and not yelled at."

"I get worried and angry when you don't return when you say you will and don't call to let me know where you are. I need to tell myself that I can't control what you do or whether you show me that you respect me. I would rather that you at least call and let me know that you are safe."

"I get scared when you say you're going to leave. I need to ask more questions to understand what you mean by 'leaving.' I want you to be honest with me and direct about how you feel."

"When the children act up I get frustrated and confused about how to be a good parent. I need to get time away for a few minutes until I cool down. I want to be open to the needs of my children."

Other examples:

Remember, you are responsible for the effort, not the outcome.

May Not Be Reproduced

WORSHEET 29   **Assertive Actions**

1. List examples of assertiveness in the role-plays:

   Scenario One What did the man do that was assertive?
   a.
   b.
   c.
   d.
   e.

   Scenario Two What did the man do that was assertive?
   a.
   b.
   c.
   d.
   e.

   Scenario Three What did the man do that was assertive?
   a.
   b.
   c.
   d.
   e.

2. What kinds of messages do you give yourself (self-talk) that stop you from being assertive?

3. What kinds of self-talk can you use to be more assertive?

4. Write two examples of situations in which you disagreed with a partner. Then list three ways you could be assertive in each situation:

   Situation One
   a.
   b.
   c.

   Situation Two
   a.
   b.
   c.

Remember, you are responsible for the effort, not the outcome.

May Not Be Reproduced

WORKSHEET 30 How Can You Be Assertive in These Situations?

Note: These are additional scenes to use when you practice assertiveness.

1. Your partner answers the phone, whispers into it for a few seconds, then hangs up quickly as you walk into the room.
   a.
   b.

2. Your partner goes to the store and is gone for two hours longer than she said she'd be.
   a.
   b.

3. You and your partner are going to a friend's new home. You wrote down the directions and address, but forgot to bring them with you. Your partner says she thinks you have gotten them lost.
   a.
   b.

4. You saw a new television that you just had to have. When you bring it home and show your partner, she explains that she just paid the bills two days ago and there was only $27 left in the checking account.
   a.
   b.

5. When you come home from work, you see a strange van parked in your driveway. As you enter the house, you hear voices coming from the bedroom.
   a.
   b.

6. Develop your own scenes:

Remember, you are responsible for the effort, not the outcome.

WORKSHEET 31   **Assertive Behavior Record**

In what ways were you assertive this week?

Date	Situation	How you felt	What you wanted	How you were assertive	How well you handled the situation	What you gained	What the other person did	Rewards you can give yourself for being assertive

Remember, you are responsible for the effort, not the outcome.

May Not Be Reproduced

WORSHEET 32   Assertiveness Strategy Plan

You can improve your assertiveness skills by planning for tough situations. Think of some tough situations that happen again and again. Fill in the chart below as you plan how you can be assertive in each of these situations. This will help you prevent abuse from occurring. Use the tips below the chart to help you plan your assertive responses.

Person involved	Possible situation	How you feel when the situation happens	What you need to do when you feel this way	What you wish would happen in the situation

Following are some tips for being assertive:

1. Use assertive body language

    - Be a comfortable distance from the other person.
    - Take deep breaths before reacting.
    - Take a time-out first, if necessary.
    - Avoid pointing, staring, and standing over someone.
    - Speak in a clear voice.
    - Use "I" statements.

2. Communicate assertively by using the formula below:

    When you (say or do) _____ ,

    I feel _____ .

    When I feel this way I need to _____ .

    I want the situation to be different (or I want you to) _____ .

3. If the other person does not agree with you, answer the following questions for yourself:

    - What can I control about this situation or person?
    - What do I feel now?
    - What do I need to do now?
    - How should I take care of myself in this situation?

Remember, you are responsible for the effort, not the outcome.

May Not Be Reproduced

Goals

Upon completing this activity, participants will:

1. Understand the obstacles to relaxing and reducing stress in their life.

2. Develop a plan to reduce stress and maintain some relaxation in their life.

3. Understand how and why to develop a support system for relaxation.

4. Teach themselves to reduce stress and relax.

Relaxation Plan (Worksheet 33)
Relaxation Log (Worksheet 34)

◆◆◆

Introduce relaxation as a part of self-nurturing and self-maintenance. Discuss how stress affects us and the types of stresses that are healthy and unhealthy.

Ask the men to turn to Worksheet 33, Relaxation Plan, and respond to all of the questions on the worksheet. Give them fifteen minutes, and explain that they can leave a question blank if they don't have any ideas. After they have completed their worksheets, discuss the first question, "What are some obstacles that prevent you from relaxing?" Ask the following questions:

• Is this obstacle a self-talk message?

• Is this obstacle part of your environment or are you in an atmosphere that prevents you from relaxing?

• Do you have certain rules about relaxing that if not followed can become obstacles?

Next, ask each person to list his five major stresses and whether those stresses are positive and healthy or negative and unhealthy. Suggest that they focus primarily on those areas that are negative. Have them rate each negative stress on a scale of one to ten, one being the least stressful, ten being the most stressful.

Brainstorm stress-reducing activities that they're already practicing. Write them on the chalkboard. After collecting all those ideas, add new ideas to the list. Talk about barriers to using these techniques. Help them develop a plan that includes who they can talk to about stresses and where they can go to relax, whether it is for a few minutes, a few hours, or several days.

List the ways that they can work off their stress, anxiety, or tension. Discuss sports or other activities that do not turn into an abusive or tense time for them, or in which they put undue pressure on themselves. (For example, some men who play in league sports are so fiercely competitive that the game only adds to their stress level.)

Finally, ask the men to state some of the self-talk statements that help them relax. (Examples of such statements include "I can stay calm," "I am only responsible for me," and the use of relaxing images.) List these on the chalkboard. Discuss how these types of statements aid relaxation and the type of support they should seek out to continue this positive self-talk.

Explain that they will be completing a Relaxation Log (Worksheet 34) during the next two weeks. They are to choose a number of activities from their relaxation plan and monitor them using the chart provided. Point out that this chart will be a record of the things they have done to take care of themselves.

Follow-Up

During the follow-up session, talk about what was helpful in doing this exercise, discuss their concerns about lack of relaxation, and how they might address those concerns. Discuss further how lack of relaxation is connected to abuse, control, and power issues. Explain how feelings of powerlessness and hopelessness can result from stress, tension, and anxiety, and that they compensate for those feelings by abusing or trying to control other people. However, there are better options to coping with stress, and relaxation is one of these. Emphasize that the forms of activities they use to relieve stress may change over time.

1. *Some of the men may not view relaxation as a major issue in their lives nor connect it to their abusive behavior.* When you introduce this activity, address their hesitation or lack of interest. Emphasize that relaxation can help prevent them from being abusive. Allow for differing opinions and give support, particularly for those who are willing to investigate this issue.

2. *Help them see how stress can be both healthy and unhealthy.* Allow each man to define healthy and unhealthy for himself. Some men may find crowds relaxing and energizing (thus healthy), while others need quiet time alone. Support their differences and reinforce the underlying commonality: They are developing a plan to take care of themselves, and that feels good. If, however, the men pick risky activities that they call relaxing, such as going to a bar, it's important that you point out the risks attached to those activities.

3. *Point out that attending the domestic abuse group may itself be a major stress in their life.* Week after week, the group forces them to remember their issues related to violence and abuse, and brings up feelings of guilt and shame. Coercion into attendance (through a choice between jail or treatment) adds to the anxiety and stress of being in the group. Help the men understand that talking with the group about these stresses can help alleviate them.

4. *Chemically dependent men may find relaxation difficult.* Some of these men have adjusted to life as a roller coaster ride. In fact, some of them may feel that trying to relax is itself stressful. Help these men develop a great variety of relaxation techniques, both through activity as well as through some sort of self-talk, meditation, or spiritual activity that is appropriate for their recovery program.

5. *It's important that the men identify people with whom they can discuss their stresses, as well as places they can escape to for relaxation.* The men tend to generalize these parts of their relaxation plan. Encourage each group member to name who they have talked with and where they've gone in the past. Help them dream about what relaxes them, so they can look at the one- to two-minute escape as being a place in their own minds, while the longer relaxation destinations are more real, such as visiting a friend, going out of town, and so forth.

6. *Help them see the connection between their relaxation plan and the goal of remaining abuse free.* Their decisions about abuse, as well as their problem-solving skills, will be affected by the way they take care of themselves. Help them recall their perspective before joining the abuse group, and consider how the lack of a relaxation plan may have affected

them in the past. Emphasize that as long as they take care of themselves, which is the focus of this program, they will be taking care of others (friends and loved ones) in the process. Their responsibility for their behavior and what they can control in their own lives is at the heart of this relaxation activity. It may help to review some of their past successes with relaxation, and also some of their red flag signals for abuse. Help them keep on track by encouraging them to develop a relaxation plan that is simple and doable, rather than a complex one that is destined to fail.

Notes, comments, and observations:

Participant's Workbook Sample

Goals

In this activity, you will:

1. Understand the obstacles to relaxing and reducing stress in your life.

2. Develop a plan to reduce stress and maintain some relaxation in your life.

3. Understand how and why to develop a support system for relaxation.

4. Teach yourself to reduce stress and relax.

WORKSHEET 33	Relaxation Plan

1. What are some obstacles that prevent you from relaxing?

2. Name the five major stresses in your life:
   a.
   b.
   c.
   d.
   e.

3. List the activities you do that are relaxing and help you relieve stress:

4. What are some other things you would like to do for relaxation?

5. Who can you talk to about the above stresses?

Name	Phone #

6. Where can you get some time away for:

1-2 minutes	1-4 hours	1 day to several days

7. List the ways you can work off stress, anxiety, and tension:

8. List some self-talk statements to help you relax:

May Not Be Reproduced

WORKSHEET 34   Relaxation Log

During the next two weeks, make a commitment to _____ number of relaxation activities. Record your progress on the chart below:

Date	What you did to relax	For how long	Stress level before relaxing (1-10)*	Stress level after relaxing (1-10)*

*1= least stressful, 10 = most stressful

May Not Be Reproduced

Goals

In this activity, participants will:

1. Increase their understanding of the options available to build a self-care system.

2. Develop a self-care maintenance plan.

3. Identify aspects of their lives they want to begin (or continue) to nurture for the sake of their health.

4. Begin a process of daily self-care, rather than living from crisis to crisis.

Required Worksheets

Self-Care Assessment (Worksheet 35)
Self-Care Options (Worksheet 36)
Self-Care Plan (Worksheet 37)

Format

Ask the men to turn to Worksheet 35, Self-Care Assessment, in their workbook. Explain the importance of taking care of oneself daily and the need to (at least initially) plan this care. The worksheet provides space for the men to give examples of how they currently care for themselves, how often they do so, and how adequate their care is. Give them fifteen minutes to fill in one or two examples of their current self-care strategies. Explain that they won't be discussing these examples at this time.

Offer some analogies to help the men understand the importance of self-care for preventing a recurrence of abuse. For example, cars will not run or work well unless they are maintained. Athletes cannot perform at their peak efforts unless they stay healthy and maintain their skills.

Explain that a plan consists of many options. Not all the options need to be used all the time, but having a variety of options for self-care provides flexibility and reduces stress.

Ask the men to turn to Worksheet 36, Self-Care Options. With the group, brainstorm options for each of the aspects of self-care. Write these ideas on the chalkboard. At the same time, have the men record, in their workbooks, those ideas that fit their needs.

Next, have the men turn to Worksheet 37, Self-Care Plan. Ask each man to focus on at least two of the self-care categories and to specify the length of time they will monitor those categories. A week is a good starting point. Explain that they will be reporting on their progress during a follow-up session. Explain that for each man support for maintaining the plan may come directly or indirectly. Some men may actually ask friends to talk directly about self-care while they are together, while other men may prefer just being with friends without direct discussion about stress or other self-care concerns.

Follow-Up

At the follow-up session, have each man report on his progress. Ask some of the following questions:

- How closely were you able to follow your plan?

- Are there other categories you need to focus on in the future?

- What prevented you from doing what you said you were going to do?

- What ways can you get support to follow your plan?

Discuss how it feels to have a self-care plan and what has been helpful about having a plan. Suggest a second, longer period for monitoring their self-care plan. Be sure to provide a follow-up session to discuss their progress, accomplishments, and any needed alterations in their plan.

After they have monitored themselves twice, have the group members fill out another Self-Care Assessment Worksheet. Discuss the changes and progress they have made. Point out that they have become more sensitive to taking care of themselves. Ask about the differences and similarities in the two assessments and the implications for what they should work on in the future.

Issues

1. *Men usually don't think about self-care.* This can be a refreshing and hopeful activity that helps them reframe the concept of taking responsibility for themselves. Maintaining a self-care system is being responsible. Not all sessions need to be heavy and directly confrontational.

2. *Many of the men may already be involved in some self-care.* Often, the ways we take care of ourselves are assumed or left unnamed. When the self-care system is identified, it can become a strong tool for preservation, flexibility, and comfort. In other words, a man who knows he'll be

out fishing in a few hours is better able to deal with the stress of a job. A man without a plan will simply pile stress on top of stress. Affirm the options the men are already using in their self-care systems. Encourage them to consider some of the "brainstormed" options even if they have failed in the past.

3. *Some men resist this activity.* They may say a self-care plan is stupid or useless. Or they may see this activity as piling up more work. Focus on what they already are doing to take care of themselves. Encourage them to challenge themselves by focusing on one or two other areas.

4. *Some men may feel overwhelmed.* Point out that they don't need to work on everything at once. They do need to choose one or two critical areas and decide how much effort to put into them. Help these men develop a personalized plan.

5. *Men who are chemically dependent or who are used to living from crisis to crisis may think self-care is boring.* It's possible that these men are more comfortable with life on the edge as opposed to a more stable way of life. Provide your observations and ask other members who may have dealt with these feelings to talk about their growth process. It may be appropriate for you to be direct and confrontational with your opinion that they may try to find excitement through unhealthy forms such as arguments and fights unless they have less self-destructive alternatives planned. Listen carefully to these men's concerns; often they want to be satisfied with a self-care plan, but the things they've tried haven't caught their interest. Encourage them to try more of the brainstormed options, perhaps with another group member.

6. *Encourage the men to develop many options for maintaining their self-care plan.* Discuss the need to be flexible with the plan rather than rigidly expecting only one way of fulfilling a self-care need. Explain that rigid expectations are a setup for frustration if circumstances prevent, for example, running or working out. Strongly encourage as many options for each category as possible.

7. *Practice is the key to success with the self-care plan.* Failure to practice the plan will lead to frustration, anger, powerlessness, and burn out. Keep the men motivated by praising their progress when they complete the monitoring exercises. This is also the reason we encourage them to develop their own plan and pick their own focus areas—to keep them invested in their plans.

Let them know that they will act the way they practice. Explain that it is helpful to identify the times they should have followed through, or areas they want to improve, because this is part of the process of understanding their own needs. Be patient with the choices that they make for themselves. They may not progress as far or as fast as you wish. If you become frustrated, evaluate your expectations and review your goals for each of the men and the group as a whole.

Notes, comments, and observations:

Participant's Workbook Sample

Goals

In this activity, you will:

1. Increase your understanding of the options available to build a self-care system.

2. Develop a self-care maintenance plan.

3. Identify parts of your life you want to begin (or continue) to nurture for the sake of your health.

4. Begin a process of daily self-care, rather than living from crisis to crisis.

WORKSHEET 35   Self-Care Assessment

List some ways you take care of yourself. Then rate how well you take care of yourself in each of the following categories.

Category	What you do now	How often	Rating (1–5)*
Self-Reward & Self-Talk			
Social			
Relaxation			
Work			
Exercise			
Nutrition			
Assertiveness			
Fun			
Spiritual			
Emotional			

* 1 = not enough; 3 = adequate; 5 = extremely well

May Not Be Reproduced

WORKSHEET 36   Self-Care Options

Physical Exercise Plan
How can you work off energy or anxiety in a constructive way? What activities or sports will help?

Relaxation and Stress Reduction Plan
What can you do to relax and think clearly?

Nutrition Plan
What foods and eating patterns will help you relax and think clearly?

Self-Reward & Self-Talk Plan
What positive things can you tell yourself that will help you think clearly? How can you reward yourself?

Spiritual Plan
What are your spiritual aspects? Where can you go to get more support for your spirituality? Who are your spiritual role models, and how can you spend time with them?

Social Plan
What sort of events do you (or could you) attend with friends that are positive and healthy for you? Who are the people in your life that are supportive, encouraging, and positive influences?

Emotional Plan
What ways can you better recognize your feelings? Who can you get support from to be emotional? Who can listen to you express your feelings? How can you see these people regularly? If these people are unavailable, what can you do to support yourself?

Fun Plan
List ways to have fun that are healthy and do not hurt others. Pick three of these that you can do for yourself or with others in the next two weeks.

Assertiveness Plan
What situations regularly come up at work, with your partner, or with your children that require you to be assertive? How can you prepare to be assertive in these situations? (See Worksheets 28-32 for information on how to practice assertiveness.)

WORSHEET 37 — Self-Care Plan

#		
WORKSHEET 37		**Self-Care Plan**

List at least two self-care categories you will focus on for the next _____ weeks:

1.

2.

Use the chart below to record your progress in these categories. For each category you choose, record the date and what you did to take care of yourself. For example, if you chose "Physical Exercise," you might write Monday: run 30 minutes; Tuesday: lift weights, and so forth.

Date	Physical Exercise	Relaxation & Stress Reduction	Nutrition	Self-Reward & Self-Talk	Spiritual	Social	Emotional	Fun	Assertive-ness

List where or from whom you will get support for maintaining your self-care plan:

1.

2.

3.

4.

May Not Be Reproduced

Building and Maintaining a Support System

Goals

In this activity, participants will:

1. Increase their awareness of issues they need to deal with after leaving the program.

2. Increase their awareness of support people and organizations.

3. Develop a support system of people and other resources to deal with a variety of issues.

Required Worksheet

Building and Maintaining a Support System (Worksheet 38)

Format

One week before this activity, ask the men to fill out Worksheet 38, Building and Maintaining a Support System, in their workbooks. Explain that they should try to fill in every part as completely as possible. Tell them they will be sharing some of their responses with the group, but that other than that, the information is for them only; they should keep it in a place where they can refer to it quickly, especially in times of emotional distress.

When the group meets, lead a discussion that takes the men through their responses to the worksheet. Ask how they decided which people are only for small talk, which people they can talk about their life with, and which people they can trust with personal information. Talk about the kinds of family, work, and other issues they may want to address after leaving the group. Ask if they thought of any other issues that are not mentioned and who they would contact for those issues. Have each group member state at least one group or organization and one person he will meet with for support after the program ends.

Hand out a local resource list with contact information for other issues that they may want to focus on. Explain that these are important issues to explore if and when appropriate. Not everyone is ready to examine these issues in the same way, same time, or to the extent someone else may.

Issues

1. *This activity will help the group members realize that they have almost completed the program.* Remind them of your availability after the group sessions are completed, as well as other resources to deal with their ongoing abuse issues. Discuss the feelings of loss, grief, and fear that stem from leaving the group.

2. *Some men may resist filling out this worksheet.* For a variety of reasons, group members may attempt to simply state their responses. Encourage them to record their plans and support network even if they believe their plans will change the next day. Explain that you will make copies for your files in case they lose theirs.

3. *Encourage group members to keep this worksheet readily available.* In times of crisis, it is difficult to identify people or resources that may be helpful. The written reminder will help, and they may add more alternatives as they review their worksheets.

4. *Point out that there are other ways for them to take care of themselves.* If they are busy taking care of themselves, they may spend less effort on the need to control someone else. Early on in this exercise, the issue of controlling oneself needs to be discussed.

5. *Prepare a list of local resources.* If you are in a small town or a city with few places men can go for help, this may be difficult. In that case, help group members be creative about how to get the support they need. Suggest they use the group list of phone numbers, look for ways to plan to visit some friends or family on a regular basis, develop new friendships, or attend community education classes to expand the number and types of people they have contact with.

◆◆◆

Notes, comments, and observations:

Goals

In this activity, you will:

1. Increase your awareness of issues you need to deal with after leaving the program.

2. Increase your awareness of support people and organizations.

3. Develop a support system of people and other resources to deal with a variety of issues.

WORKSHEET 38 Building and Maintaining a Support System

1. List all the people you work with, spend time with, or have contact with in your daily life:

2. Draw a circle around those people with whom you are comfortable making small talk.

3. Next, draw a box around those people with whom you are comfortable talking about your life.

4. Now draw a triangle around those people you can trust with personal information.

5. List all the people from above who you can call for social reasons or in times of crisis. List the names in order of preference, from people you are most likely to call to people you are less likely to call.

6. List the people or organizations you can contact to discuss the following issues:

Family Issues

Divorce	Relationships	Parenting	Childhood experiences

Job Issues

Coworker relationships	Job-related conflicts	Employer relationships

(continued)

What are some other issues you need to focus on? Look through the list below. Circle the ones that apply to you and add any that are not included.

- Chemical dependency
- Smoking
- Adult child of an alcoholic
- Family of origin
- Abuse survivor
- Shame
- Building and maintaining relationships
- Nurturing yourself
- Values
- Boundaries
- Self-esteem
- Overly dependent
- Sexism
- Honesty
- Eating
- Emotional health
- Sexuality
- Spirituality
- Intimacy
- Parenting
- Recreation

Where can you get help with these issues?

7. List groups and organizations that you now (or plan to) participate in as part of your support system.

	Name of group	Issue	Time it meets	How often it meets
a.				
b.				
c.				
d.				
e.				

8. List the people you will meet with as part of your individual support system.

	Name	Phone #	How often
a.			
b.			
c.			
d.			
e.			

Cluster 5

Personal Development

Personal Values

Goals

In this activity, participants will:

1. Better understand and define their personal values.

2. Identify and understand how they model these values for other people.

3. Explore the degree of agreement between their values and their partner's values

4. Explore what to do when their values are not in agreement with someone else's values.

Required Worksheet

Personal Values (Worksheet 39)

Format

Discuss the definition of values. Explain that values are qualities that you appreciate in other people. Values are ways of thinking about things and viewing the world, and they are guidelines we use to react to situations. Discuss how we learn values and the people who are most likely to affect what values we learn. Discuss some of the following value questions relative to relationships:

- Why is it okay to hit a woman?

- When is it not okay to hit a woman?

- Is it okay to put down a woman?

- Is it okay to disgrace somebody from another culture or race?

- Is it okay to disgrace another human being?

- Why do we treat people at work differently from the way we treat people at home?

Help them examine the values that support their answers to these questions. Discuss the fact that values are different for everyone, and differences in values are normal, just as differences in opinion are normal. Point out differences in values about money, work, school, and partners.

Show them that their own values change over time; for example, tastes in music often change from childhood to adolescence to adulthood. Ask how their values about how a wife (or partner or girlfriend) should act have changed since they were adolescents.

Discuss media heroes, childhood heroes, and how they have affected the men's values. Ask how the media influence their values about how they treat women and how they treat people from other cultures.

Ask the men to turn to Worksheet 39, Personal Values. Explain that they'll have fifteen minutes to complete the worksheet and that they will be discussing their statements in the larger group when they reassemble.

After fifteen minutes, bring the men back together to discuss their answers. First, ask each man to name whom he admired and the five qualities of that person. Then lead a discussion about the similarities among people the men admire.

Next ask them to state the five values that they listed on their worksheets. These values could relate to anything, from relationships, to music, to sports, to politics. List all their responses on the chalkboard as they share them, regardless of the value stated. Next, have them discuss the ways that they demonstrate their values to other people. Ask how their behavior reflects the values they've expressed.

Have them name the one value they would teach their children, why they chose that value, and how they model that value for their child. After everyone has responded, ask the following questions:

- Why is it important to accept the fact that your children have different values?

- At what point is it wrong for your child to have a value different from yours?

Reassert that just as they have changed values about music, they can change their values about how they treat other people, including their domestic partner. This is true no matter how much violence they have seen or how streetwise they feel they are. Note that some values have a higher priority in our lives than others, and some values are less prone to change over time. For many people, these types of values come from religious or ethical systems. These values also grow from specific cultural roots.

Ask for examples of values from men of different racial, ethnic, or cultural backgrounds, or from different regions such as urban and rural. Emphasize that people with differing religious, cultural, and regional values can live and work side by side and can even become close friends despite these differences. Ask the following questions:

- Are there certain people whose differing values are acceptable because of who they are?

- At what point does it feel like someone is pushing their beliefs on you?

- How do you react when someone starts to push their beliefs or try to make you believe a certain way?

Finally, point out that certain values are embraced by the majority of people in our society. These values usually are expressed in the form of laws. In particular, our society has a value that we do not assault each other. Point out that these men have broken that value by assaulting their partners.

Shift the discussion to the next set of questions on the worksheet. Ask the men to volunteer answers regarding to what degree they think their partner (or ex-partner) shares the same five values they listed as their most important values. Repeat this discussion around their children's values. Finally, ask whether everyone in the same family should have the same values.

To conclude the discussion, ask for suggestions on how to react when someone expresses an opinion or acts on a value system that differs from theirs. Deepen the discussion by asking for assertive, nonviolent responses when a person tries to force a foreign value system on them.

Issues

1. *It may be difficult for some men to fully grasp the concept of values.* Try to make values as concrete as possible. Describe values as qualities in ourselves that shape our view of the world and how we act. Examine how, ultimately, these values are reflected in our behavior. For instance, if we believe that something is an object that we can move around, much like a basketball, football, or chair, then we have some control over it and can do what we want to it. If we see other human beings as objects, then we will think it is okay to control them, just as we would control a basketball. Help them see how they may have been acting out this value when they abused their partner.

2. *Some men may try to engage you in an argument about your value system.* Allow them to talk about their differences in values. Ask a few questions to help them gain insight into their choice of values: Is that a value they like? Are they comfortable with it? Do they always want to hold on to it? Point out that some people have vowed never to do or say what their parents did or said to them, and yet find themselves years later repeating their parents' patterns. Help them recognize that we select certain values simply because they are what we've grown up with, and that values can be consciously changed. Avoid engaging in an argument about whose values are better.

3. *Some men will resist listing their five values, or have difficulty naming any values at all.* Ask them to name five beliefs about anything, including music, work, sports, money, family, friends, and religion.

4. *Talk about specific ways that they demonstrate these values or beliefs.* One way many men can identify with is how they protect themselves based on their view of other people. Ask streetwise participants to talk about how they size up a person they see walking down the street— what do they look for, and why? Help them see how these safety-oriented decisions are based on value judgments they have made.

5. *Ask them to be very specific about the degree of agreement between their five values and their partner's values.* Are they exactly the same, somewhat similar, or totally different? As they talk, help them recognize if they tend to discount their partner's values. If a man says he just doesn't know his partner's values, have him focus on what he *thinks* those values are, based on her actions. Understand that he may be misrepresenting her because he is angry with her. For example, he may say she is promiscuous when in fact she is not, and he has been unfaithful.

6. *Use the question about their children's values to help them understand the developmental phases of children.* Point out how children often adopt their parents views exactly until adolescence, and then test those views by acting in opposition to them (rebelling). Help them avoid expectations that their children are just small adults who will understand and follow adult value systems.

7. *At length, discuss how other people's values can be different from theirs.* Have the men talk about many different situations, from a variety of backgrounds and perspectives. This may be a good time to do some role-plays, such as asking them to argue from the perspective opposite to theirs.

8. *Remember that you are not necessarily imparting values, but you are modeling your value system for the men.* Point out that agreeing to disagree is a positive quality and that this quality can be nurtured. Discuss the principle of controlling oneself versus trying to control someone else. Relate this principle directly to the fact that other people have their own values, and we can't control whether they change those values.

◆◆◆

Notes, comments, and observations:

Goals

In this activity, you will:

1. Better understand and define your personal values.

2. Identify and understand how you model these values for other people.

3. Explore the degree of agreement between your values and your partner's values.

4. Explore what to do when values are not in agreement.

WORSHEET 39   **Personal Values**

1. Name one person you admire most:

2. List five qualities you admire most about that person:
   a.   d.
   b.   e.
   c.

3. List five of your personal values:
   a.   d.
   b.   e.
   c.

4. Describe how you show each of these values to other people:
   a.   d.
   b.   e.
   c.

5. If you had to choose one value to teach your children, which would it be? Why?

6. How do you model this specific value to your children or others?

7. What are your partner's opinions related to the five values you listed? Does (or did) your partner agree with you?
   a.   d.
   b.   e.
   c.

8. What are your children's opinions related to the five values you listed?
   a.   d.
   b.   e.
   c.

(continued)

WORKSHEET 39 (continued)

9. Do other people's values have to be the same as yours? Why or why not?

10. How can you react when someone has an opinion different from yours?

May Not Be Reproduced

Goals

In this activity, participants will:

1. Better understand the effects of parenting.

2. Look at how adults appear to children when violence has occurred in the home.

3. Define discipline and punishment and develop a plan to use disciplining behaviors.

4. Better understand the effects of violence on children.

5. Learn about what can be done for children who have witnessed abuse or who have been abused.

6. Develop a set of parenting values.

Parenting and Discipline (Worksheet 40)

Introduce parenting and briefly discuss the meaning of parenting with the group. Have the men turn to Worksheet 40, Parenting and Discipline, and ask them to answer the first two questions. Then ask each group member to make one statement about each of their children, including the child's first name. After everyone has talked about their children, discuss the similarities of the statements made about the children. This will help the men better understand themselves as parents, and also help them begin to relate to each other as caring parents.

Ask the group members to imagine themselves as one of their children. (Ask group members who do not have children to remember themselves as children.) Discuss how children see the world and what it might feel like to be a child. After this brief discussion, section off six columns on the chalkboard. At the top of the first column write, "What the children have seen, heard, or know has taken place at home." Ask the group members to talk about what their children, or what they themselves as children, saw while they were growing up in their home. Even if they think the child was sleeping, ask them what the child may have overheard or may have learned from other people.

The next column should be labeled, "How they might have felt." Here, it may help to refer the men to the Feelings Words Worksheet in their workbook. Have them list all the feelings that a child would have about all of the events in the first column.

In the third column, write, "How the children have acted." Record their responses and descriptions of the children's behaviors in response to the events listed in the first column.

In the fourth column, write, "What the children need." Have the group review the first three columns and then ask them, "In light of these three columns, what do the children need?" Write all their responses on the chalkboard.

In the next column, write, "What we can provide." (Ask those men who do not have children to think about what their caregivers could have done for them as children.) Finally, write in the sixth column, "What we can't provide." Record their responses. This helps the men gain a realistic view of what they can and can't do to fulfill the needs of their children, especially if the men are not custodial parents.

Discuss the connections between the ideas in each column on the chalkboard and any conclusions that group members can make about these ideas. Help the men focus on their limitations as caregivers as well as the need for them to get support as caregivers. Give information about how they can nurture themselves—for example, in parent support groups, through books, and with friends. Help them discuss parenting as a learning process that includes mistakes from which they can learn. Discuss the importance of what they are already providing as parents and the many other ways they could nurture their children.

For men who have been violent, another important aspect of parenting is an increased understanding of the difference between punishment and discipline. Explain that all of us have had unique learning experiences in respect to becoming a parent. There is a tendency for us to repeat these experiences even though we may state our opposition to the style of parenting such experiences represent. (For example, ask the men how many of them thought as children, "I'll never do that to my kid when I grow up," only to repeat the behavior of their parents.)

Introduce the terms, punishment and discipline. Write "Punishment" on the chalkboard. Brainstorm ideas for the definition and intent of punishment. Look for or contribute some of the following words or phrases: abusive, vengeful, indirect, may initially change unwanted behavior, relieves the parent's frustration, is really for the parent's benefit.

Make another column on the chalkboard and write "Discipline." Brainstorm ideas on the meaning of this word and its intent. Some of the words or phrases to look for: teaching, nurturing, nonabusive, caring, is for the child's benefit, is clear and direct, gets the point across, is safe and nonthreatening.

Next, help the group members focus on the differences between the two words. Help them understand discipline as a helpful, structured, and productive way of learning from experience. In contrast, punishment is really the use of the child's behavior as an excuse to hurt, abuse, or seek revenge, and is unproductive.

Ask the men to turn to Worksheet 40, Parenting and Discipline. Have them copy down the brainstormed terms and definitions of punishment and discipline, and then give them ten minutes to complete the lower half of the worksheet. Let them know that you will be asking them to share two things that they want their children to learn, and two ways that they can help them learn those things.

Issues

1. *Without a doubt, spanking will be brought up by group members and will need to be addressed within the group setting.* It will be important for you, as the counselor, to develop your own perspective on spanking and corporal punishment as a way of disciplining. We recommend that you maintain a strong line against any form of physical punishment. (The research indicates that spanking and similar forms of punishment are less efficient and effective than alternative nonviolent options.) Allow the group members to discuss their views and cultural perspectives. At some point during this activity, clearly state your perspective that corporal punishment should not be used. Challenge other group members to look at spanking from the viewpoint of a child. Try to avoid power struggles and convincing group members that they need to change their perspectives. At the same time, challenge them to develop creative noncorporal alternatives to punishment.

2. *Parenting is a volatile subject for many of the men.* Some of them were abused or witnessed abuse as children, and some have abused their own children. In both cases, they may come to realize this only through the course of these group sessions, particularly this parenting activity. Allow the group members to discuss their situations as children. State that it's not okay for anyone to be abused and that any abuse they experienced as a child was not their fault. Similarly, any abuse their children have experienced is not their children's fault.

Some group members will argue that because they were abused, they turned out to be good people. It is important to validate that they did not deserve abuse, and to point out that they may have turned out to be good people, in spite of their having been abused. Some of them may state that their parents had no other way to control them as children, except to be abusive. They may say that abuse (or strict discipline) is what they needed in order to behave. Discuss the reality that as children, they were powerless to deal with situations in which they were victims. Point out that their parents were not powerless in handling these situations and had some other options available. State that abuse was used to try to control the situation and change their behavior when they were children.

3. *Often, group members will say they do not want their children to experience the same things that they themselves experienced as children.* This becomes a harsh reality to many of the group members as they discuss this issue. Their feelings of guilt and shame over what their children have experienced may prevent them from fully expressing their views about what their children have seen and heard and how they may feel. It is important for you to have the group members talk about these feelings and how the feelings may affect their behavior toward their children. Assist them in focusing on ways that they can teach their children alternatives to being violent.

4. *During the discussion on punishment and discipline, there is a tendency for group members to justify the way they punish their children by calling such punishment "discipline."* Discuss the alternatives to physical punishment and point out that there is *always* an alternative to punishment or abuse. Children can learn more from the use of discipline than they can from the use of punishment. Ask the group to generate a list of alternatives to using punishment. Include rewards and positive feedback to children. Help them to find creative ways to reward children besides food or money. Help them develop lists of positive ways of giving rewards. Also help them list the rewards they, as parents, receive for using discipline instead of punishment.

5. *Some men tend to talk about their anger toward their children in much the same way they talk about the anger towards their ex-partners.* Affirm that the feelings may be similar, but the child is not the ex-partner. Use the part of this activity in which you encourage the men to see the world as a child to emphasize what the children need and how the men can be a good model for them.

6. *Some men will point out that in this world, you can't completely protect children from violence.* Talk about how it feels to know that violence is out there and that their children are vulnerable to it. Discuss how they can minimize the risk to their children. Brainstorm alternatives that they have as parents or caregivers to help their children develop positive problem-solving skills to avoid being violent.

7. *While doing the children's experiences chart, many men realize that the violence their children have witnessed has affected them.* Give the men plenty of time to discuss their feelings as well as what they can and can't do to help their children. Try to avoid long discussions that blame the system or the children's mother, as the men have no control over those people or systems. Help them focus on how they can help their children cope with the effects of the violence they witnessed.

8. *Some men may minimize the need to develop a discipline plan with their children.* Men who do not have children may minimize the need to have a discipline plan. It is helpful for these men to talk about their own family of origin experiences and help them relate those to other children in their lives, such as nephews and nieces or children of their current partner. Also, some men say they don't need a plan because their children are too old. It is important to model nonviolent behavior, no matter how old their children are. Emphasize the need to look at a discipline plan as something for them to do, not necessarily something for their children to do. As caregivers and parents, their reactions to their children will ultimately teach these children how to react to situations in the future.

9. *During this activity, many of the men will realize that their own family of origin experiences are still affecting them today.* Encourage these men to continue to investigate and explore this area of their life with appropriate individual counseling. Some major issues that need to be further dealt with outside of the group include neglect, abandonment, and sexual abuse as a child.

10. *Encourage parents and caregivers to examine all their options, even in stressful situations.* The men may attempt to corner you by describing impossible situations, just as they did when you were presenting the philosophy of the program; they are looking for your permission to be abusive in some situations. Instead, emphasize the need for them to look at their alternatives in dealing with their children, rather than focusing on feeling stuck. Allow them to discuss their feelings at length and what "stuck" means. The fewer options they give their children, the fewer options they will have when providing discipline.

11. *Some men will challenge your authority as a parent.* This is similar to the "you don't know what I've been through, so don't tell me anything" mind-set. Whether you have children or not and whether you decide to tell the group this or not, challenge the group members to learn from each other and to listen to what others are saying. Admit to your limitations and inability to answer all questions. Try to avoid long justifications or statements to establish your authority on the subject, as this may lead to power struggles.

Notes, comments, and observations:

Participant's Workbook Sample

Goals

In this activity, you will:

1. Better understand the effects of parenting.

2. Look at how adults appear to children when violence has occurred in the home.

3. Define discipline and punishment and develop a plan to use disciplining behaviors.

4. Better understand the effects of violence on children.

5. Learn about what can be done for children who have witnessed abuse or who have been abused.

6. Develop a set of parenting values.

WORSHEET 40   Parenting and Discipline

Once a parent, always a parent.

1. What does it mean to be a parent:

2. How do you demonstrate care for your child(ren):

3. List the differences between punishment and discipline. Which one is hurtful? Which is for teaching? Which is more helpful and respectful of children? What prevents you from using alternatives to punishment?

Punishment	Discipline

4. In what ways can you provide your child more discipline?

(continued)

WORKSHEET 40 (continued)

5. Use the behavior change chart below to list some of your children's behaviors that require discipline. In the other columns, write the natural and logical consequences of their behavior, and any rewards they might receive by switching to the desired behavior.

Behavior Change Plan

The behavior	Natural consequences	Logical consequences	What you want them to do instead	Rewards

6. Questions to ask yourself as a parent:

   a. What can I control about my child's behavior?

   b. What form of discipline does my child respond to positively?
   Verbally
   Through natural/logical consequences
   Through rewards

   c. How do I feel when my child misbehaves?

   d. How do I usually react when my child misbehaves?

   e. What support and resources do I need when disciplining my child?

   f. What can I do for myself when disciplining my child?

   g. What rewards do I receive for using discipline with my child?

   h. What negative consequences do I receive for using punishment with my child?

Goals

In this activity, participants will:

1. Increase their awareness of the dynamics of partner relationships.

2. Better understand and prioritize their needs or expectations in a relationship with a partner.

3. Increase their sense of personal responsibility for their side of the relationship.

Relationships (Worksheet 41)

Discuss the definitions that group members have for the term "relationship." Examine the differences in types of relationships. For example, how does a work relationship differ from a partner relationship? What is a friendship as opposed to a family relationship? Do different rules apply to these different relationships?

Ask the men to turn to Worksheet 41, Relationships. Explain that visualizing relationships can help us learn about them. Instruct the men to draw their current or most recent relationship with a partner using two shapes. Have them use the proximity of the shapes to symbolize how their relationship with their partner was when it began. Then ask them to draw two more shapes showing how their relationship looks today. Give them five minutes to do this and explain that they will be describing their drawing to the rest of the group.

Have each group member briefly describe his pictures. After everyone has spoken, discuss the similarities and differences in the two pictures. Ask what themes were common to the pictures. Also ask what the form and size of the shapes indicated.

Accept their drawings as being real for them. What they draw is important and is a good way for them to begin to understand their relationship with their partner. Don't judge their drawings or even suggest that their pictures should be different.

Explain that you see relationships generally taking four forms. Draw the following four pictures on the chalkboard:

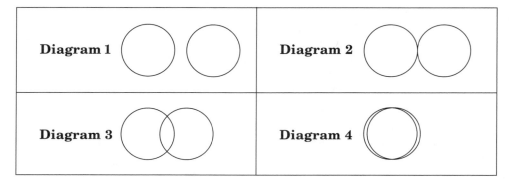

Discuss the similarities between these drawings and those of the group. Discuss each diagram at length and ask some of the following questions:

- How does it feel to be in a relationship like this?

- What are some real-life examples of what this kind of relationship (diagram) is like?

- What are each person's goals for and outlook on this relationship?

- What aspects of the relationship are shared?

- How does person A react when person B begins to pull away or tries to get space?

- Who is responsible for person A's circle?

- What would happen if person B decided to leave the relationship entirely?

- To what extent might person A prevent person B from leaving the relationship?

- Why would person A try to prevent person B from leaving?

Explain Diagram 1 as symbolizing a relationship that is at a distance. Very little, if anything, is held in common or shared between the two people. Ask the group some of the following questions in regard to Diagram 1:

- How would it feel to be in this kind of a relationship?

- How much commitment does each person have to this relationship?

- How much investment does each person have in this relationship?

- How would you describe this relationship?

- Would this be a comfortable relationship for you at this time in your life?

- If person B left this relationship, how might person A feel?

Explain Diagram 2 as a relationship that meets, connects or shares one need, characteristic, or activity. There continues to be little commitment or investment by either person. Have the group members discuss and describe this type of relationship. Ask some of the same questions you asked regarding Diagram 1, as well as the following:

- How much trust is required in this relationship?

- If person B left the relationship, how much of person A would remain?

- Would a potential loss of that much mean a lot to person A?

Explain Diagram 3 as a relationship that shares some activities, and fulfills some needs of each person. Have the group members describe how it would feel to be in this relationship. Ask some of the following questions:

- What are some of the benefits?

- What are the drawbacks to this relationship?

- What if person B wants to pull out of the relationship to where the relationship looks more like Diagram 1 or 2?

- If person B pulled back, what would person A do, feel, or think about person B?

- How much of person A would be left if person B left the relationship entirely?

- What might person A do to prevent this loss from happening?

Explain Diagram 4 as a relationship that is all-encompassing. All activities, time, and just about every aspect of each person is tightly meshed with the other—so much so that it is difficult for one person to live without the other. Discuss how it would feel to be one of these people. Ask all of the questions from above as appropriate.

Finally, ask which of these four relationships the men would feel the most comfortable in at this point in their life. Discuss their responses and reasons.

Explain to the group that they have fifteen minutes to complete and answer questions three through eight on the Relationships Worksheet. Explain that they will be talking about what they have written with the rest of the group.

After fifteen minutes, discuss their responses to the questions. Assist them in examining issues related to control, loss, grief, and dreams about a relationship.

Ask the group members to discuss which of the four diagrams might be considered the most destructive (Diagram 4). Help them examine how a person in a relationship resembling Diagram 4 can move to a more healthy situation.

Ask them what information they need to know in order to move toward a healthier relationship. Help them see that they must specifically identify and prioritize what characteristics they want in a partner. Have the group brainstorm these characteristics while you record them on the chalkboard.

Ask the group some of the following questions:

- What does this list tell you about your attitudes toward your partners?

- How realistic is it to believe there is one person to fulfill all of these requirements?

- How would the lists differ if your partners were asked what they wanted?

- Would this list be as overwhelming or difficult for you to fulfill as for your partners?

Explain that the group will now agree upon and prioritize five character-istics that are the most important to them. Allow the group to make the decisions, and mark each selected characteristic with a star. After they select the five characteristics, ask some of the following questions:

- What is important about these five qualities?

- If a partner only had these five characteristics, would that satisfy all your needs?

- If you could add three more characteristics to the priority list, what would they be?

- Can you get all your needs and wants met by one person?

Have each group member summarize their learning from this activity by responding to the final section of the worksheet (questions 9-17). Give them ten minutes to complete the worksheet and explain that they will be talking about what they have written with the rest of the group. Before getting into the large group, have them break into groups of two or three. Explain that they should discuss their responses with the small group. After everyone has talked in their small groups, bring them together and have them discuss their responses.

After everyone has talked, ask the following questions:

* What are some similarities in what you have learned about your relationships?

* Where do you take it from here?

Finally, discuss how the men felt about this activity.

Issues

1. *Often the men come into this session looking for ways to fix their partner or fix their relationship.* Give them plenty of time to discuss what "relationship" means to them. Ask those men who are no longer in a relationship to consider their past relationships, and remind them that it is highly probable that they will have a relationship in the future. Help each man focus on his role in a relationship and the fact that the only person he can control is himself. This is a good time to review the 100% rule.

2. *Some men may refuse to draw or visualize their relationship.* Explain that this is not an art contest and they will not be graded on their pictures; the only goal is their own growth and better understanding of themselves. Support their use of any type of illustration that fits for them.

3. *Some men may be reluctant to discuss their picture.* Allow them to see some other men participating and sharing their pictures. If a man continues to refuse to participate, refer to your policy regarding nonparticipation in group sessions. Most of all, avoid power struggles, and if possible, give yourself time by asking that this person speak next week, or asking this person at what point they would be willing to share this information.

4. *Don't judge the "correctness" of the men's illustrations or choice of words.* When you begin to talk about the four diagrams on the chalkboard, explain that these are ways that *you* see relationships. The drawings they did on their own sheets of paper are not incorrect, but the ones that you draw on the board are ones that fit for others as well as yourself.

5. *Most men can relate the diagrams to a specific relationship they've had.* Particularly when you describe the fourth (enmeshed) diagram, many men may see some parallels to their current or former relationships. Discuss, at length, how it feels when their partner wants to change to a relationship that resembles Diagram 3 or 2 when they themselves want to maintain the relationship as portrayed in Diagram 4. This is a major issue for many men; help them talk about their need to control and keep the relationship. Most men experience grief and loss when

their partner wants to change the nature of the relationship or end it altogether. Because these men don't like these emotions, they try to hang onto (and control) the relationship at all costs.

6. *Some men also talk about terminating their relationship before the partner terminates it.* This way, they feel in control of the relationship and avoid feeling abandoned or rejected. Give the men the opportunity to talk about these feelings and about what actions they would take in order to prevent someone from rejecting or abandoning them.

7. *When men first start to examine what they want in a relationship, they often focus on beauty or sex.* When brainstorming the characteristics they want in a relationship, accept all responses. Avoid judging any responses or statements.

8. *Be sure that they work as a group to prioritize the five characteristics that are most important to them.* This will be difficult for many of the men, as they may have already made their choices, but press them to make a *group* decision. This process can be frustrating for you as the counselor, because you want them to come up with the decision and they are either hesitating, not participating, or having difficulty coming to some decisions. Try to stay out of their interactions until they have made a group decision; only they, as a group, can determine how long this process will take.

The purpose of this activity is threefold. First, it gives the group another opportunity to make group decisions while you observe the process and dynamics. When the exercise is completed, it may be appropriate for you to give your observations to the group—for example, who seemed to lead, who stayed in the background, who helped facilitate consensus, and so forth.

Second, this activity helps men learn about their own wants in relationship to those of other men. Some men, upon hearing the desires of other men, will realize that their own desires are not strange or odd. As they list characteristics, they see the many ways women are perceived in relationships and learn that while not all men want the same things in a partner, there are similar attitudes and themes in what they want.

Finally, this part of the activity allows men to begin to safely and honestly question their views of an "ideal" partner. This technique allows for more discussion among the group members and seems to increase their insight into their expectations of a partner.

9. *It is paramount to discuss whether they can get all their needs met by one person.* Have them talk about how it feels to *want* to get all their needs met by one person. Ask if they can realistically find all the characteristics on the chalkboard in one person. Discuss other people who could help meet their needs, including themselves. In many ways, this exercise can lead into a discussion of intimacy and sexuality.

10. *The last page of the worksheet helps them integrate everything they've learned in this activity.* Encourage them to answer the questions with specifics: what type of person they feel safest with, what signals they need to be aware of, and who they can control in a relationship.

Notes, comments, and observations:

Participant's Workbook Sample

Goals

In this activity, you will:

1. Increase your awareness of the dynamics of partner relationships.

2. Better understand and prioritize your needs or expectations in a relationship with a partner.

3. Increase your sense of personal responsibility for your side of the relationship.

WORKSHEET 41   Relationships

1. You can learn a lot about relationships by drawing a picture of them. Relationships can be shown by how close or far apart two circles are drawn. Using two circles, draw what your current or most recent relationship with a partner looked like when it began. Label your circle with an "M" and your partner's circle with a "P."

2. Now draw how this relationship looks today:

3. What has changed? What has stayed the same?

4. What does it feel like when your partner wants to move her circle away? How might you react? Who is responsible for your circle (your side of the relationship)?

5. What might you lose if the relationship changes? What might you gain?

6. What are your dreams about how your partner relationships should be?

7. How have you felt when you've realized these dreams would not come true?

8. How can you grieve the losses for changes in your relationship?
   - Who you can talk to:
   - Where you can go:
   - What you can do:
   - What self-talk you can give yourself:

9. List the characteristics you look for and want in a partner (the ideal partner will be...):

10. How many of these expectations can one person meet?

(continued)

11. List the five characteristics you would rate as most important in a partner. (In other words, what are the five qualities you could not do without.)
    a.
    b.
    c.
    d.
    e.

12. Why are these five important to you?
    a. Because:
    b. Because:
    c. Because:
    d. Because:
    e. Because:

13. If you could add three more, what would they be?
    a.
    b.
    c.

14. What type of person do you feel safest with?

15. What and who is the only thing you can control about the relationship?

16. List the things you've learned about your relationship that will change the way you behave with partners in the future:

17. What has been helpful about looking at your expectations of a partner?

May Not Be Reproduced

Intimacy, Sexuality, and Sensuality

Required Worksheets

Intimacy, Sexuality, and Sensuality (Worksheet 42)
Intimacy Needs Scale (Worksheet 43)

Format

Introduce the terms sexuality, intimacy, and sensuality as normal human needs that require attention in our lives. Put a column for each of these terms on the chalkboard. Ask the men to contribute definitions for each using examples, feelings, and situations. Ask the men to turn to Worksheet 42, Intimacy, Sexuality, and Sensuality. Ask them to record the ideas you've written on the chalkboard onto their worksheets. Suggest that they add to the list as they think of new ideas. Finally, discuss obstacles to meeting these needs, and have them record some of these obstacles in their workbooks.

Next, shift the discussion from present-day needs to the development of their perceptions about these needs. Ask how and from whom they first learned about these needs. Ask the men to talk about how they were supposed to show intimacy when they were in junior high or elementary school, and how the rules for showing intimacy differed with various people. Have them list these messages about showing intimacy on their worksheet.

After exploring the origins of the messages men receive about intimacy, give the group five minutes to list ways that their being abusive has been an obstacle to intimacy. Ask them to list at least five ways. After they have done this, have each man state two ways in which his abusive behavior was an obstacle to getting his needs met.

Ask the men to turn to Worksheet 43, Intimacy Needs Scale. The scale names eight types of intimacy. Explain these for the men:

- *Social intimacy* has to do with relationships with friends and others.

- *Emotional intimacy* has to do with expressing and talking about feelings.

- *Intellectual intimacy* has to do with the sharing of information between people.

- *Physical and recreational intimacy* has to do with sports or related physical activities.

- *Sensual intimacy* has to do with the actual senses—touch, taste, smell, sight, and hearing.

- *Affectional intimacy* has to do with getting the affection that one needs.

- *Sexual or genital intimacy* has to do with sexual stimulation.

- *Spiritual intimacy* has to do with their relationship with nature or a deity, depending on their beliefs.

There are other columns that can be added, such as parental intimacy. Encourage them to add any other columns that fit their situation. Ask them to use the chart to rate where they are now with each of these needs, as well as where they would like to be. Encourage them to be completely honest.

After they have completed their worksheets, draw the chart on the chalkboard and ask each man to tell you where he has placed an "N" (to indicate where he is now) on each of the columns. After everyone has contributed, look at the chart on the chalkboard and talk about what it tells them—does it seem like everybody is very similar, or are they different. Which needs aren't getting met for most men?

Repeat this process with the "W"—what the men want. Look at their responses and discuss the themes. Ask the men how they plan to reach their goals, what they need in order to get those goals met, and what resources they need to know about in order to get those needs met.

To wrap up the activity, ask questions such as :

- What has been the importance of this activity?

- What has been helpful about discussing sexuality, intimacy, and sensuality?

- What more do you need to know about yourself in regards to these three areas?

- What should your current partner or a new partner know about these three areas?

- Who can you talk to about any one of these three areas?

- What does it feel like to talk about these issues?

- How often do you talk about these issues outside of this program?

- How will this discussion help your relationship in the future?

Issues

1. *Intimacy, sexuality, and sensuality are often not addressed in men's domestic abuse groups.* It is important to address these issues as they are real needs for these men. Their inability to express these needs or lack of understanding of their options for meeting them has two effects. First, they may behave inappropriately toward their partner in trying to get these needs met, and this can be a setup for choosing to act abusively. Second, without this information, the men have less of an understanding of how they have affected their partner.

   Before presenting this material, it is important that you have a firm grasp of where you stand on these issues. We recommend that you develop your own list regarding your personal sexuality, intimacy, and sensuality needs. Don't underestimate the impact of your own perspective on the group. Be aware of your own biases. If they become obstacles to your clients or result in you becoming frustrated with the men's responses, seek support and consultation from other professionals.

2. *Some men see no practical reason to talk about these particular issues.* Ask them to express their concerns and feelings about discussing intimacy, sexuality, and sensuality. Discuss any options that they might have for participating in the activity, depending on your policy for the program. If they seem to have difficulty coming up with ideas for intimacy needs while in the group, give them some suggestions and ask them where those suggestions might fit into the exercise.

3. *Help them develop a list of obstacles to getting their needs met.* These obstacles may include their job, schedule, feelings, friends, children, other family members, abusive behavior, or perhaps some history related to the relationship. Help them understand that these obstacles are not insurmountable and can be dealt with; sometimes what appears to be an important priority can be set aside in order to get an intimacy need met.

4. *When discussing the history of how they learned about these terms, help the men remember both the messages they received and how they felt about those messages.* Examine as many ways as possible that they were allowed to show intimacy or prohibited from showing intimacy.

Explore how these rules applied to their relationships with other boys, with girls, with parents, and with other adults.

5. *Help them recognize how their abusive behavior has been an obstacle to getting their needs met.* Spend time with the worksheet question, "List the ways that your abusive behavior has been an obstacle to getting your needs met."

6. *Use the Intimacy Needs Scale to raise the men's awareness of their unmet needs.* After your discussion of unmet needs that are shared by most men, shift the focus to how they can develop better ways of getting their needs met. Emphasize that talking about these needs and seeking noncontrolling ways to meet them is superior to taking what they want through abuse.

7. *Intimacy, sexuality, and sensuality are difficult topics for men to talk about.* Help each man understand as best he can how these topics apply to him and his situation. Discuss where else they might talk about these issues, and where they might get support for finding a healthy balance in getting their needs met.

Notes, comments, and observations:

Goals

In this activity, you will:

1. Understand the definition of intimacy, sexuality, and sensuality.

2. Increase your awareness of your needs in each of these three areas.

3. Better understand the barriers to meeting these needs.

4. Develop new possibilities and alternatives for meeting these needs.

WORKSHEET 42   Intimacy, Sexuality, and Sensuality

1. List examples and ideas to define the following terms:

Intimacy	*Sexuality*	*Sensuality*

2. Now write examples of how you get these needs met:

Intimacy	*Sexuality*	*Sensuality*

3. What are some of the obstacles to getting these needs met?

4. Who first taught you about these terms?

5. When you were growing up, how were boys supposed to show intimacy?

6. When you were growing up, how did you deal with your needs to be sexual?

7. List five ways that being abusive has been an obstacle to getting your intimacy, sexuality, and sensuality needs met:
   a.   d.
   b.   e.
   c.

8. List five things you can do to meet your intimacy, sexuality, and sensuality needs without being abusive:
   a.   d.
   b.   e.
   c.

WORSHEET 43 — Intimacy Needs Scale

Put an "N" on the scale to show where you are *now*. Put a "W" on the scale to show what you *want*.

Type of Intimacy:	Social	Emotional	Intellectual	Physical & Recreational	Sensual	Affectional	Sexual or Genital	Spiritual
High 7 need								
6								
5								
4								
3								
2								
Low need 1								

Adapted from Marilyn J. Mason, Ph.D., Licensed Psychologist, Department of Family Social Science, University of Minnesota Medical School, and author of *Making Our Lives Our Own* (Harper San Francisco) 1986 and coauthor of *Facing Shame: Families in Recovery* (W.W. Norton) 1986.

Self-Esteem and Empowerment

Goals

In this activity, participants will:

1. Increase their self-esteem.

2. Better understand which areas of their life they can control.

3. List specific activities that lead to a sense of increased self-worth and empowerment.

Required Worksheet

House of Self-Worth and Empowerment (Worksheet 44)

◆◆◆

Format

Ask the group members to state activities and aspects of their lives that are particularly important to them. As they speak, generalize their ideas into subject areas and write them on the chalkboard. For example, if someone volunteers "meeting my buddies at the bar," you can make that a category of social life, intimacy with others, or nurturing. Or if someone suggests "league bowling," you could make a category for relaxation, competition, recreation, hobbies, or social life. There are many possible categories; the ones we usually generate include relaxation, social life, relationships, partner relationships, job, parenting, and spirituality.

When they seemed to have exhausted their lists of ideas, draw a house on the chalkboard similar to the one you created in the activity, House of Abuse, (page 52). Divide it into seven to nine rooms. Put one of the categories you generated into each room. One room at a time, ask them how they will take care of this area of their life. When the rooms are full, ask some of the following questions:

- How does it feel to look at this house?

- What is the result of doing these things to take care of yourself?

- What is the purpose of taking care of yourself or doing these activities?

- What do the rooms support?

- How are these rooms interrelated?

- How do the rooms strengthen each other?

On the roof of the house, write *self-worth* and *empowerment*. Discuss these terms and how taking care of oneself can lead to a sense of self-worth and a sense of being empowered or in control of oneself.

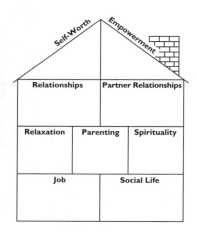

House of Self-Worth and Empowerment

Discuss how feelings in the basement continue to exist, just as they existed in the House of Abuse. Some of these feelings are very unpleasant, but the way they are acted out in the House of Self-Worth and Empowerment is different from how feelings are acted out in the House of Abuse. In the House of Abuse, feelings of anger may be acted out through violence, abusive language, or manipulation. In the House of Self-Worth and Empowerment, the same feeling may be dealt with through exercise, assertive confrontation, or a time-out.

Ask the men to turn to Worksheet 44, House of Self-Worth and Empowerment. The house is sectioned into nine rooms. Explain that they will have fifteen minutes to fill in the house as it fits for them, after which time they will share their responses in the group. In other words, each man will list nine aspects of his life (one category for each room) that are important to him. Then he will list the ways he is currently taking care of himself, as well as ways he plans to take care of himself in the future. Finally, he should answer the two questions on the second page of the worksheet.

When the group has reassembled, instruct each person to pick two rooms to talk about. After all the group members have responded, ask some of the following questions:

- How are the responses similar?

- What were some of the similar ways to take care of yourself?

- Who is in control of following through on these plans?

- Who can take the credit for taking the action and accomplishing these tasks?

Emphasize the issues of being responsible for oneself and controlling oneself. Discuss at length how it felt to examine their lives in this activity. Discuss options for follow-up on this activity, such as a monitoring worksheet or an update on progress in each room.

1. *Some men may question the importance of this activity.* Point out that positive self-worth is at the foundation of choosing a violence-free life. Often, men are not aware of or will not give themselves credit for the amount of work they already do to react nonviolently. This exercise helps them identify some of these solutions as well as develop even more options to build their self-worth.

2. *Guide their listing of important aspects of their lives by reframing specific issues into more general ones.* For example, work is part of a larger category of employment and career. Once this is a heading for a

Issues

room in the house, talk about the specifics of taking care of oneself in the employment area: consistent employment, regular attendance, punctuality, competence, performance of required tasks, and so forth.

3. *Encourage each man to pick the nine categories that best fit his life.* If a man chooses categories that do not seem applicable, guide him into more realistic choices. The choice of inappropriate categories may be an indicator that he wants to focus on someone other than himself.

4. *Encourage the men to be creative in naming the ways they can take care of themselves in each room.* Avoid judging their ideas on how to take care of themselves. If an idea seems truly impractical, let the group point this out. As they talk about their individual rooms, they will teach each other even more options. Suggest alternatives if an idea is potentially dangerous.

◆◆◆

Notes, comments, and observations:

Participant's Workbook Sample

Goals

In this activity, you will:

1. Increase your self-esteem.

2. Better understand which areas of your life you can control.

3. List specific activities that lead to a sense of increased self-worth and empowerment.

WORKSHEET 44   House of Self-Worth and Empowerment

1. Label each room in the house below with an aspect of your life that is important to you. (Some examples include *job, family, recreation,* and *friends.*) Then fill each room with specific examples of what you currently do or plan to do to take care of yourself within that category. (For example, under *friends*, you might write, "Continue to keep in touch with my friends.")

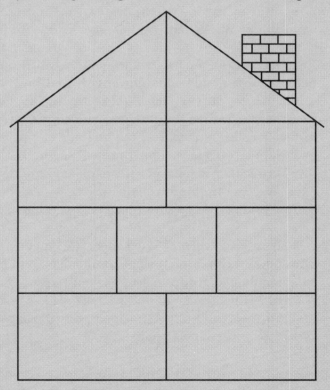

2. What are your feelings when you look at your life this way?

3. What positive actions can you take to fill up these rooms?

May Not Be Reproduced

Angry
Feelings

Goals

In this activity, participants will:

1. Become more aware of their feelings of anger, related feelings, and where those feelings originate.

2. Identify varying intensities of anger and the feelings related to anger.

3. Develop a plan to express anger appropriately.

Required Worksheets

Anger and Abuse (Worksheet 45)
Anger Escalation Log (Worksheet 46)

Format

As a group, discuss the meaning of anger. Talk about other words that may be similar to anger, such as pissed, mad, upset, and frustrated. You may want to use Worksheet 10, Feelings Words, to find more synonyms.

Suggest that anger has different intensities, and explore the difference between low anger, medium anger, and high anger, and how the men might behave during each of these types of anger. Discuss what they want to accomplish when they are experiencing low levels of anger compared to higher levels of anger. Use the analogy of a pressure cooker on a stove to explain the effects of unexpressed anger; if the steam is kept in, the pressure cooker will eventually explode. Explain that they must be able to express anger appropriately before they explode. Explain that anger is a feeling and there is a difference between anger and abuse.

Ask the men to turn to Worksheet 45, Anger and Abuse. Give them five minutes to draw a picture of their anger and of their abuse. When you reassemble the group, discuss the differences and similarities in these pictures. Have the men identify how it feels to be angry and to appropriately express their anger, as opposed to using abuse or power and control tactics to express this anger.

Continue to work through the worksheet. Have the men fill it out as they talk about how they let people know that they are angry. Discuss the difference between directly expressing anger and expecting that someone can read your mind. Ask them how they tell coworkers, bosses, or friends that they are angry. Talk about the risks, difficulties, and obstacles to expressing anger directly to these people.

Next, ask how they let their partners know that they are mad. Compare the ways they express anger to their partner with the ways they express it to other people. Help them see that they don't abuse other people when angry, but they will abuse their partner when angry. Relate this expression of anger to power, control, and consequences. When they are with employers, their job may be in jeopardy and other consequences may occur, so they don't express anger abusively. But in a partner relationship they may believe they can get their way without as many consequences, and so they choose to exercise power and control over their partner.

Next, ask them what they do (or know that others do) when they get upset or angry with themselves. Do they call themselves names, put themselves down, or even hurt themselves physically? Have them list examples that are appropriate to their situations. Discuss how such thinking often leads to feeling depressed, overwhelmed, and hopeless.

Discuss the symptoms of depression and what resources may be available if some men describe depression-related problems that interfere with the rest of their life. (Some indicators include sleep disorders, poor appetite, and an overall sad outlook.) Note that sometimes, depression is covering up angry feelings.

Finally, discuss specific healthy ways that they now use or could learn to use to express their anger. Help them develop many options. Some suggestions you can contribute, if the men are not forthcoming with ideas, include:

- Talk with someone you trust.

- Go fishing.

- Go to a movie.

- Be direct and assertive in your communications.

- Exert some energy by working out or taking a walk.

- Give yourself positive self-talk about controlling your own behavior.

- Take deep breaths and count to ten.

Ask the men to turn to Worksheet 46, Anger Escalation Log. Ask them to select two feelings related to anger and monitor those feelings for the next week. Tell them that they will be reporting from their logs in the next session.

Follow-Up

Write the following headings on the chalkboard, using the same format as the Anger Log: Feeling; Situation; Intensity of feeling; Other feelings during the situation; Your thoughts during the situation; What you did when you felt this way; Who you talked with about the situation; and How you felt after talking about the feelings. Ask group members to talk about what they logged during the past week, and write their responses in the appropriate column. Encourage them to report on all aspects of the log, both positive and negative.

Ask the group what they have learned about their anger as a result of this exercise. Discuss the differences in intensity of anger and the multitude of options that there are for expressing anger. Remind them that anger does not need to be expressed in an abusive, controlling, or manipulative way. Emphasize that abuse also arises from many other feelings, such as hurt, depression, powerlessness, helplessness, or frustration, and that it is important to identify all of these feelings in order to deal with them, rather than lumping them all under the category of anger. Finally, suggest that they repeat the Anger Escalation Log another week to continue to identify these feelings of anger.

Issues

1. *Often, men are confused by the discussion of anger. Some men see anger as synonymous with abuse.* Give examples of differences. Differentiate these terms by describing anger as a feeling and abuse as an action.

2. *After being arrested or experiencing other consequences of their abusive actions, many men feel that anger is not an acceptable feeling.* Explain that anger, like all feelings, is a signal we need to attend to. Point out that anger varies in intensity, and does not always have to result in rage. Finally, reinforce that anger does not have to be acted out through abusive behavior.

3. *There are many feelings related to anger that need to be explored.* These include powerlessness, frustration, rage, fear, hurt, revenge, depression, humiliation, and many others. (See the activity, Escalation Signals, page 63, and Worksheet 10, Feelings Words, page 68.) Men who abuse are often overwhelmed by the sheer number of feelings they experience and use anger as a way to describe it all. It is important that

you help them identify the feelings related to anger. Encourage them to talk about different types of anger, as well as how these different types feel. This will enable them to better understand and express their feelings.

4. *Keep in mind that anger is not the root cause of abuse.* Men abuse to maintain power and control in a relationship, not because they are angry. Abuse is a technique used to satisfy the need to control and maintain power in a relationship. But anger *is* a factor in abuse, and as such requires attention.

5. *Emphasize that anger is a healthy feeling.* Often, anger is viewed as a negative experience. Help them to see anger as a normal feeling; it can be a signal that they need to find ways to take care of themselves.

6. *Help the men understand how their thinking may differ in situations where they feel angry at work, with friends, or with a partner, even though their anger may be equal in intensity throughout.* Discuss the reasons behind these different thought patterns. Examine how their behaviors differ with these people as well. Ask how they are able to control their anger with one type of person and not with another.

7. *Discuss how they express anger toward themselves.* Some men choose self-destructive ways of expressing anger such as using alcohol or other drugs, while others choose healthy ways such as exercising or talking with friends. Explain that anger toward oneself is normal. Talk about depression and how long it takes for group members to pull themselves out of the feeling of anger toward themselves. Review the symptoms of depression if necessary, and make referrals for individual counseling as appropriate.

8. *Help them plan specific, healthy ways that they can express their anger.* This may relate directly to the responsibility plan they developed in the activity, Responsibility Plan, page 70. However, it should be more specific to coping with feelings of anger. Assist the men in devising a Healthy Anger Plan, if the group appears willing to commit to it. Include the examples of healthy choices to express anger, ways to get support when angry, a rating system to quickly assess the intensity of anger, and how to evaluate one's own behavior after a situation has occurred which triggered an angry response.

9. *During the follow-up discussion of the Anger Escalation Log, have them be as specific as possible about the situation and the corresponding intensity of feeling.* Again, emphasize that intensity is different for every situation and that not every situation results in a high level of anger. Use this log as a tool to discuss the positive aspects of what they have done to cope with anger rather than trying to control the situation and manipulate other people.

◆◆◆

Notes, comments, and observations:

Goals

In this activity, you will:

1. Become more aware of your feelings of anger, related feelings, and where those feelings originate.

2. Identify varying degrees of anger and the feelings related to anger.

3. Develop a plan to express your anger appropriately.

WORKSHEET 45 — Anger and Abuse

1. Anger and abuse are two different things. Draw a picture of each.

Anger	Abuse

2. When you get angry at friends, supervisors, or people at work, how do you let them know you're mad?

3. How do you let your partner know you are angry at her?

4. What are the differences in how you show anger toward other people and how you show anger toward your partner?

Other people	Partner

5. What are the similarities in how you show anger toward your partner and toward other people?

Other people	Partner

6. What do you do when you are angry at yourself?

7. List specific unhealthy ways you have expressed anger at yourself or others:

8. List specific healthy ways you have expressed your anger:

Worksheet 46 — Anger Escalation Log

List two feelings related to anger. Monitor these feelings on this chart for the next week.

Feeling #1 _____

Situation	Intensity (low, medium, high)	Other feelings during this situation	What you were thinking during this situation	What you did when you felt this way	Who you talked with	How you felt after talking about the feelings

Feeling #2 _____

Situation	Intensity (low, medium, high)	Other feelings during this situation	What you were thinking during this situation	What you did when you felt this way	Who you talked with	How you felt after talking about the feelings

May Not Be Reproduced

Goals

In this activity, participants will:

1. Better understand grief and how it affects their behavior.

2. Increase awareness of their hopes and dreams about a relationship.

3. Understand what dreams they have lost and how they lost them.

4. Understand how loss of dreams may affect their behavior.

5. Gain support for talking about loss and developing new hopes and dreams.

Loss of Dreams (Worksheet 47)

Most people are familiar with the grief and pain caused by the loss of a loved one, but they may not recognize that grief can also accompany the loss of dreams. Open the discussion by talking with the men about grief and its stages. Although there seems to be no apparent order to the feelings that accompany the loss of a relationship or loved one, people usually experience anger, denial, blame, some bargaining, guilt, depression, and ultimately acceptance. Even after working through all these feelings, they may reoccur with decreasing intensity during the years following a loss. Help the men understand that these feelings are normal. Point out that if the thoughts or feelings become overriding—possibly influencing destructive behavior—some intervention is necessary.

After describing grief at the loss of a loved one, shift the focus to the dreams the men have had about relationships. What expectations does society have of them and their families? What did their own family expect? What kind of relationship did they want to create?

Talk about the feelings they had when they realized these dreams couldn't be accomplished, or when circumstances beyond their control thwarted their dreams. Connect the feelings of anger, sadness, and frustration with the feelings that people experience when someone dies. Help them see that in a very real way, the loss of a dream is like losing a loved one. Point out that they can have similar feelings about other losses: the loss of a pet, the loss of a job, even the loss of a favorite car or other material item.

Ask them to turn to Worksheet 47, Loss of Dreams. Explain that they will have fifteen minutes to complete the worksheet and that they will be discussing their responses in the large group. After they have completed the worksheet, reassemble the group and discuss each item.

Ask each man to show what he drew to illustrate his feelings about the loss of an object, the loss of a person, and the loss of a dream. As he shows the three pictures, ask him to comment on the similarities and differences in the three experiences. Ask about the intensity of feeling regarding each loss. Find out if he objectified people in the process, if he minimized or denied his feelings, and if these feelings of loss built (or might build) toward an explosion at himself or someone else. Help the man see the connections between the feelings he has when someone else "causes" the loss of a dream (for example, his partner leaves him) and the intense feelings surrounding his attempts to prevent such a loss.

Next ask the men to share some of their dreams, values, or beliefs about relationships with a partner. As they talk, list their responses on the chalkboard. Next, ask them to talk about some of the dreams they have lost in regards to relationships. Ask some of the following questions:

- How does it feel to lose these dreams?

- What dreams do you still have that you may lose?

- How has your behavior been affected by the loss of these dreams?

- How do you show this loss to other people?

Discuss how and where group members can get support for their grief over lost dreams. Ask them who they can talk with about their losses, and how they can develop new dreams for their current or future relationships. Discuss the feelings that occur with grief and loss, and point out that these feelings are different for each person and with each circumstance. Ask the men to describe their own feelings about loss, how they tend to react to it, and what helps them cope with feelings of loss. Explain the risk of depression associated with loss, and how to recognize it.

Finally, explore the possibility that their partner (or future partner) may have different dreams from their own. Ask the men if it's okay for people in a relationship to have different dreams about that relationship, and to what extent those dreams can differ within a healthy relationship. Revisit the principle that one can only control oneself, and point out that this principle is also true for their dreams about the future.

Close the discussion by commenting on the hopefulness of this activity. Ask them to think about how they can use this information to grieve the loss of old dreams so they can move on to creating new dreams.

◆◆◆

Issues

1. *Some men don't see grief and loss as a priority in their lives.* Discuss the emotional consequences when a loss is not grieved. Also help them see that a fear of grief can lead them to be controlling. That is, their fear of the pain of losing their relationship and the dreams associated with it may motivate their decision to abuse their partner to keep her from leaving.

2. *If men resist drawing their feelings about grief, remind them that this is not an art contest.* Ask them to make the illustration as simple or complex as they like. The only goal is to show their feelings.

3. *Help them talk about the names of their feelings and how they show these feelings of loss to others.* Many men receive nonverbal support from other men by simply being together or doing an activity together with no reference to the particular loss at all. Help them understand and identify the kinds of nonverbal support that they get from their friends.

4. *Ask the men to be specific about their dreams for relationships.* Help them examine some messages about relationships: what their parents and friends told them; what they learned by watching their parents. Ask the men what parts of those messages they'd like to act on and what parts they want to do differently. Help them rephrase the negative messages—those elements they don't want to repeat—into positive dreams. For example, the negative message, "My partner is there to serve me" could be rephrased "My partner and I are in this together and I will look for ways to share in making the relationship work." The message, "I need to have control and take 100 percent responsibility for all my family members" could be rephrased "I can contribute to my family's well-being by finding ways to take care of myself."

5. *Some men may already be experiencing depression.* Teach the group about depression, and when to seek help for it. Make appropriate referrals for individual counseling, when appropriate. Seek professional support and supervision when needed.

Notes, comments, and observations:

Participant's Workbook Sample

Goals

In this activity, you will:

1. Better understand grief and how it affects your behavior.

2. Increase your awareness of your hopes and dreams about a relationship.

3. Understand what dreams you have lost and how you lost them.

4. Understand how loss of dreams may affect your behavior.

5. Gain support for talking about loss and developing new hopes and dreams.

WORKSHEET 47   Loss of Dreams

1. List people or things you have lost during your life:

2. Draw the following three pictures:
    a. How you feel when you lose an object.
    b. How you feel when you lose a person.
    c. How you feel when you lose a dream.

3. How do you show these feelings to others?

4. Who can you tell about these feelings?

5. What are some dreams, values, or beliefs about how your relationship with a partner should be?

6. Have you lost some of these dreams about relationships? Which ones?

7. How does it feel to lose these dreams?

8. What dreams do you still have that you may lose?

9. How and where can you get support when you lose a dream?

10. What new dreams do you have about your relationship or future relationships?

Cluster 6

Evaluations

Midterm Group Evaluation

Goals

In this activity, participants will:

1. Give support, input, concerns, and observations of progress to each other.

2. Identify, review, reevaluate, or add to their personal goals for the program.

3. Receive constructive suggestions for areas to focus on in the remaining group sessions.

4. Increase their skills in talking directly with peers about abuse.

Required Worksheet

Midterm Group Evaluation (Worksheet 48)

Format

Use this activity at about the midpoint of a short-term program or every quarter for programs lasting one or more years. Ask the men to turn to Worksheet 48, Midterm Group Evaluation. Explain that they will have a few minutes to think about and respond to the first two questions on the worksheet, after which they'll share answers with the rest of the group. When the group is ready, ask for a volunteer to begin.

You have several options for the next part of the exercise, depending on time limitations, counseling style, group composition, and the degree of group participation. Regardless of which option you choose, start by asking the volunteer to read his answers for the first two questions. Then ask the group to give him feedback using one of the three options described below.

Option One

Ask the man next to the speaker to state a strength, a way the speaker has helped him or the group, and a concern or issue to focus on in the remaining group sessions. Continue around the group until everyone (including you) has told the speaker one strength and one concern.

Option Two

Ask for volunteers to state a strength and a concern about the speaker until everyone has contributed.

Option Three

Leave the floor open for volunteers to state a strength and a concern, but do not require everyone to share. Make sure you always share your perceptions.

Encourage the speaker to record the strengths and concerns on his worksheet. Ask that he not speak again until everyone has shared. Then he gets to have the last word. At this point, he can address specific individuals (including you) or the group as a whole.

Repeat this process until all the members of the group have had their opportunity to be the focal point. After everyone has completed the process, ask some of the following questions:

- Was it more difficult to listen to others talk about you, or more difficult to tell others your observations?

- To what extent do you agree with what you heard about yourself from other men?

- In what ways was this situation different from being in a bar with other guys?

- What made it easier to hear observations from members of the group than to hear similar observations from an acquaintance or from your partner?

- Why do you think we do this exercise?

- When you are finished with the group sessions, how will you get this kind of input from others?

- What will help you listen to the concerns or observations of others?

Issues

1. *Some men find this exercise almost as difficult as talking about their most violent behavior.* The men generally have difficulty just listening to others' observations, especially positive ones. Sometimes they try to respond after each person has shared. Respectfully ask such men to save their responses until they have the last word. These men tend to minimize the positive comments, so be sure to reinforce the positives.

2. *This activity helps the group become more cohesive.* It builds trust and encourages direct communication in a nonjudgmental, low-risk setting. As a result, men tend to feel a bond with each other. You can capitalize on this feeling for future sessions.

3. *Continue to focus on abuse and balance your supportive statements with some confrontation.* Don't let the cohesive feeling detract from your group interventions. Review your goals and expectations for the group and its members.

4. *Use concrete examples and suggestions.* The men value your observations. Be honest. Balance your concerns with examples of positive contributions or changes since the first session. As you speak, you'll

provide a model for other men's comments and suggestions to the speaker.

5. *Don't interrupt the men as they provide feedback to the speaker, regardless of whether you agree with them or not.* Sometimes it is difficult to hold on to your own comments and concerns until it is your turn to speak. Avoid jumping on those men who give judgmental feedback to the speaker. Give your response careful thought; consider how it will affect both the individual and the other group members. You will eventually get the opportunity to follow up on the comments people make.

6. *Even when you speak to only one person, you affect the others with what you share.* Remember, the group members will think about what you say. This is an opportunity to use indirect confrontations in group. When doing so, be certain that your comments fit the individual to whom you are talking.

7. *Some men may avoid sharing any concerns.* Guide their responses by asking them to provide any information that may help the speaker. But don't be too rigid about this; press them a little for an answer, then move on.

8. *Make sure the speaker gets the last word, no matter what he says.* You may have difficulty letting go, especially if what he says is negative or contradicts your philosophy. Avoid power struggles. He has heard your concerns. Trying to convince him to believe you isn't helpful at this point in the group process.

Notes, comments, and observations:

Participant's Workbook Sample

Goals

In this activity, you will:

1. Give support, input, concerns, and observations of progress to the other members of the group.

2. Identify, review, reevaluate, or add to your personal goals for this program.

3. Receive constructive suggestions for areas to focus on in the remaining group sessions.

4. Increase your skills in talking directly with your peers about abuse.

WORKSHEET 48	Midterm Group Evaluation

1. One thing you have gained from being in this group:

2. One thing that you still want to learn, discuss, focus on, or get support for in the remaining sessions:

3. List the strengths and concerns others in the group have stated about you:

Strengths	*Concerns*

4. Your last word:

May Not Be Reproduced

Final Group Evaluation

In this activity, participants will:

1. Identify the changes they have made during the group sessions.

2. Better understand the progress they have made and insights they have gained through the counseling sessions.

3. Develop a plan for continued nonviolent behavior.

4. Listen to the observations and insights of other group members.

5. Increase their understanding of the need for support and assistance to continue their nonabusive behaviors.

Required Worksheet

Final Group Evaluation (Worksheet 49)
Group Gift (Note: this is not in the participant's workbook. It is for the counselor to photocopy and distribute.)

Format

Ask the men how it feels to be in the last group session. Help them examine all of their feelings, particularly those of grief and loss. Tell them to turn to Worksheet 49, Final Group Evaluation. Give them fifteen minutes to complete the first three questions on the worksheet. Explain that they will be sharing their answers and listening to comments from other group members.

When they are ready, ask for a volunteer to share his responses to the first three questions, "Where were you in your life when you started this program," "Where are you today," and "Make a list of *specific* actions you will take to care for yourself and refrain from being abusive." Ask the man to be brief, and keep him on track as he speaks. As he addresses the first two questions, ask for specific descriptions of how he felt about his life, having to attend group, his abuse, and so forth before attending the group and now that he is leaving. With the third question, push him to make specific statements about his plans for self-care and choosing to use nonabusive alternatives.

When he is finished, ask the first man to his right to answer two questions about the man who just spoke:

•   How has this man affected you during the course of this program?

•   What concerns do you have for this man; in other words, what issues should he focus on after leaving the group?

Continue around the circle, asking each group member to answer these two questions about the speaker. Ask the speaker to record these comments in his workbook—the strengths in one column and concerns in another. After every man has spoken, the first man may respond and give his last words to the group. During his response, no one is to interrupt him or discuss anything he says. He may direct his comments toward individuals, the counselor, or toward the group as a whole.

When the first man has completed his final response, thank him for his participation and ask for the next person to respond to the three first questions. Repeat the process until everybody—including you—has had the chance to answer all three questions and get input from all the group members.

At the end of the exercise, discuss how the activity felt—what they liked and what was most difficult. Discuss the benefits as well as any drawbacks. Ask the group to comment on what they have learned about themselves and other group members through this evaluation.

While conducting this discussion, pass around another sheet, the "Group Gift," which is for all the group to contribute to. Suggest that each person sign his name and add any parting comments he wishes. Explain that the sheet will be copied and given to them as a symbol of what they have given each other. Explain that they have a choice whether to do this and that their input to other men is important.

Toward the end of this discussion, share your feelings as counselor and facilitator of the group—your feelings of loss, concerns, and observations. Wish the men well and encourage them to contact you as needed.

Issues

1. *Many men are apprehensive and concerned about the final group session.* Encourage them to talk about their feelings and concerns, apprehensions and fears. Give them time to discuss how they might be able to take care of themselves in the future and what they might do to get the support they need.

2. *Be a role model for the kinds of comments men should give each other.* Make your comments honest, direct, specific, and brief. The men will listen to how you speak and the kinds of comments you make, and follow suit.

3. *Some men say they got nothing from the program or from the group sessions.* Accept their beliefs, and don't try to convince them that they have gained something from the process. Encourage them to focus on those things that were beneficial to other group members and help

them to understand that they did have an effect on the group process. If they continue to believe that they did not gain anything from the group, talk about how their participation affected you as a counselor, and how the things they did helped other people. With the group, discuss some potential results, in months or years to come, of participating in these group sessions.

For some men, such statements are a way to take revenge on the counselor and the system. The statements may also be a way to contain their feelings of grief or loss about the group.

4. *Encourage the men to give practical, truthful observations that will benefit the speaker in the future.* Don't interrupt the men as they give feedback, regardless of your reaction. Explain to all the group members that this is not a time to be negative or abuse other people; the goal is to focus on strengths and concerns. If some men refuse to offer any input, ask them to talk about how the speaker has benefited them while they have been in group together.

5. *The speaker's "last words" are critical to the closing ritual.* The men must have the opportunity to talk honestly about their thoughts, feelings, and responses to what they have heard from the group and the counselor. Their responses should not be interrupted or interpreted. At times, this may be difficult, as they may make no sense at all, or may say something contrary to what you had hoped. In these cases, simply allow them to say their piece.

6. *Use your turn to speak to leave each man with one solid strength and one concern for the future.* Stating too many concerns may overwhelm the speaker, while not praising a strength will also discourage him. Prepare for this session by deciding what message you want to leave each man with. As you speak, talk about the recommendations you'll be making for each man's follow-up report. Be direct, and ask if they understand your major points. Keep in mind that the comments you make to one man will also influence the other men.

If appropriate, state your major concerns for this man along with ways he can address those concerns after leaving the group. There may even be times when you need to state the potential danger you see for a man or those he associates with. Such honest input is often met with understanding and respect.

7. *At times, the comments may become repetitive.* Try to encourage the men to make original and creative comments. Guide them (if needed) to comments on strengths and concerns, and away from inconsequential talk.

8. *Tell them what they can expect from you as a counselor after the sessions are completed.* Clearly state the type of follow-up you offer (if any) or other options for continuing care in the community.

9. *Leave the men with your final observations about strengths and concerns for them.* Also, give them the opportunity to tell you, as the counselor, what could be improved in the program, what they see as positive, what they gained, and what they could have worked on more.

Notes, comments, and observations:

Participant's Workbook Sample

Goals

In this activity, you will:

1. Identify the changes you have made during the group sessions.

2. Better understand the progress you have made and what you have learned through the counseling sessions.

3. Develop a plan for continued nonviolent behavior.

4. Listen to the observations and insights of other group members.

5. Increase your understanding of the need for support and assistance to continue your nonabusive behaviors.

WORKSHEET 49 — Final Group Evaluation

1. Where were you (emotionally, psychologically) in your life when you started this program?

2. Where are you today?

3. Make a list of *specific* actions you will take to care for yourself and refrain from being abusive:

4. List the suggestions you receive from other group members below:

Strengths	Concerns

May Not Be Reproduced

Note to Counselors: reproduce the "Group Gift" sheet (next page) for the men to pass around and sign during the final session.

Group Gift

We have shared a lot over the past weeks. Saying good-bye can be difficult. Thank you for your influence in my life and what you have taught me in this process. Please accept these words as a part of me to take with you, as we may never meet again:

Other books available from the Amherst H. Wilder Foundation...

What Works in Preventing Rural Violence
by Wilder Research Center

AN IN-DEPTH review of eighty-eight effective strategies to respond to rural violence. Also includes a Community Report Card with step-by-step directions on how to collect, record, and use information about violence in your community.

94 pages, softcover, ***$17*** *00*

Strategic Planning Workbook for Nonprofit Organizations *by Bryan Barry*

CHART a wise course for the future of your organization. This book provides step-by-step guidance for developing sound, realistic plans for the future. Provides instruction, case studies, worksheets, and original illustrations.

88 pages, softcover, ***$25*** *00*

Marketing Workbook for Nonprofit Organizations
by Gary J. Stern

A PROVEN, step-by-step guide to marketing success for nonprofits. This book shows you how to create a straightforward, usable marketing plan that gets results. Provides instruction, case studies, worksheets, and original illustrations.

132 pages, softcover, ***$25*** *00*

Collaboration Handbook: Creating, Sustaining, and Enjoying the Journey
by Michael Winer & Karen Ray

EVERYTHING you need for a successful collaboration. Learn how to find and keep the right people, build trust, change conflict into cooperation, and much more. Includes worksheets, annotated resources, original illustrations, a case study, and plenty of examples.

192 pages, softcover, ***$28*** *00*

Collaboration: What Makes It Work
By Paul W. Mattessich, Ph.D., and Barbara R. Monsey, M.P.H.

EVERYONE'S TALKING about collaboration, but few seem to know what it means. Mattessich and Monsey's exhaustive search uncovered nineteen principles behind this complex but potent tool. Includes a working definition of collaboration, summaries of the major research findings, detailed descriptions of each success principle, and an extensive bibliography.

53 pages, softcover, ***$11*** *95*

NO-RISK GUARANTEE
If you're not 100% satisfied with your order, simply return it within 90 days for a full refund!

Order Form

	Qty.	Price Each	Total Amount
Foundations for Violence-Free Living (counselor's guide)		$45.00	
On the Level (participant's workbook)		$15.00	
What Works in Preventing Rural Violence		$17.00	
Strategic Planning Workbook for Nonprofit Organizations		$25.00	
Marketing Workbook for Nonprofit Organizations		$25.00	
Collaboration Handbook: Creating, Sustaining, and Enjoying the Journey		$28.00	
Collaboration: What Makes It Work		$11.95	

QUANTITY DISCOUNTS	
Substantial discounts are offered on orders of ten or more copies of any single title. Please call for more information.	Subtotal
	Shipping
	TOTAL

SHIPPING

If order totals: *Add:*
$0-$30.00 $2.00
$30.01-60.00 $4.00
$60.01-150.00 $6.00
$150.01-500.00 $8.00
$500.01+   2% of order

*Rush shipment available.
Please call for costs.
Book prices subject to change.*

Ship To
Please print clearly or attach business card

Name _____
Organization _____
Address _____
City _____ State _____ ZIP _____
Phone (_____) _____

Payment Method

☐ **Check/Money Order**—Payable to: Amherst H. Wilder Foundation

☐ **Bill Me**   Purchase Order No. _____

☐ **VISA** *VISA*   ☐ **MasterCard** *MasterCard*

Card # _____

Expiration Date _____

Signature _____

Send Orders to:

Amherst H. Wilder Foundation
Publishing Center
919 Lafond Avenue
St. Paul, MN 55104

Or **fax** your form to:
(612) 642-2061 (24 hours a day)

☎ Or **phone** us toll-free at:
1-800-274-6024

Thank you for your order!